The Saga of the SAILING HILLBILLIES

"A humorous account of the sailing misadventures of a Kentucky couple."

by Floyd Tapp

Published by
Ahoy Publishing
2116 Cedar Street
Owensboro, KY 42301

Printed by
Progress Printing Co., Inc.

The Saga of the Sailing Hillbillies

Publisher's Cataloging-in-Publication
(Provided by Quality Books, Inc.)

Tapp, Floyd G.
Saga of the sailing hillbillies : a humorous account of the sailing misadventures of a Kentucky couple / by Floyd Tapp. -- 1st ed.
p. cm.

1. Sailing--Humor. 2. Caribbean Area--Description and travel. I. Title.

PN6231.S15T37 1998 797.1'24
QBI97-41529

Printed in the United States of America

Ahoy Publishing
2116 Cedar Street
Owensboro, KY 42301

What people are saying about *"Saga of the Sailing Hillbillies"*

Floyd is a real "hoot".

Lee Wilson of Century Communications.

I howled out with laughter more reading the "Saga" than any book I have ever read before.

Chris on "Maui".

I feel like I know this couple quite well after reading the "Saga". Elaine is Floyd's anchor.

Olivia on "Cheer-i-o's".

Floyd is a "kamikaze". Elaine is truly the brave one.

Ellie on "Out of Here".

I felt like I was in the boat with them on some of their harrowing experiences. Elaine and Floyd's relationship makes this a special book.

Lydia on "Tonica".

Elaine is smart for promoting herself from First Mate to Admiral. Her chances of surviving are improved tremendously.

Don on "Sea Hag".

I had goose bumps one minute and laughed until I cried the next.

Kathy at Golfland, USA.

The "Saga" reads like the "Forest Gump" of sailing.

Jason Tapp

Dedication

I dedicate this book to my father, Arthur Ray Tapp, who passed away at the age of 81 on August 5, 1996. He was beyond a doubt the most unselfish person I have ever known or heard of. He was always there with a helping hand and an open billfold. I never saw him refuse anyone. It was automatic for him to stop and help any disabled vehicle on the side of the road, rain or shine. It was as if he had a magic touch; he could almost always get the vehicle on the road again. If the disabled vehicle needed a tire replaced and the people looked needy, I've seen him go buy a tire, have it mounted and get the people on the their way and not accept a penny.

When he died, he had a little two-bedroom shingle house on a small farm and not much else. What he did have, that money can't buy, is respect and love. No one can tell me there isn't a Heaven. There has to be a Heaven for my father and people like him.

Appreciation

I thank all the friends and family who have read the little stories I wrote about our cruise and tried to convince me that they were interesting. I thank those that would not let me give up and kept inspiring me to combine those stories into a book. Without their support and encouragement, I would never have finished this book.

If there is any success in this book or anything I have ever done in my life, I owe it mainly to three people. Those three people are my wife, Elaine, and my mother and father, Pauline and Arthur Ray Tapp. Elaine, for being a good wife and going along with me, sometimes against her better judgment. My mother, for instilling confidence (undoubtedly, too much) in me that I could do anything I set my mind to and, if I worked hard enough at it, be anything I wanted to be. I was my father's son, from him I inherited my daring and boldness. An abundance of confidence combined with daring and boldness in a Kentucky Hillbilly spells misadventures. Without our misadventures, there would be no "*Saga of the Sailing Hillbillies.*"

Table of Contents

Cruising under sail is one of the finest sports. Those who take part in it pit their knowledge and skill not against a human opponent for kudos or gain, but against the sea in all its moods. ...those who love and respect the sea as they do can appreciate their reasons for cruising; the spice that a suggestion of danger lends to it; the satisfaction of working the wind and tides to their best advantage; the confidence which is acquired when a good landfall is made after a rough passage or a difficult piece of pilotage has been successfully carried out; the feeling of achievement when a strange coast or harbour has been reached under sail; and the never-ending fascination of handling and looking after a seaworthy yacht and her gear. Cruising teaches one to rely on one's judgement and skill, and it is one of the worthwhile things that can still be enjoyed by a man and woman of independent spirit, for there are no restrictions, no organizing body is needed, and the sea is open and free for all who have the inclination to sail on it and a suitable vessel for the purpose.

Eric Hiscock, "Cruising Under Sail"

Chapter 1

Our First Sail

I have been asked numerous times how anyone from Kentucky gets involved in sailing. Everything else I have ever done from pool hustling to professional motorcycle racing has all been my doing. I blame this sailing thing on my wife of thirty-plus years, Elaine. Her Uncle Tommy, who is now deceased, and Aunt Julia have a home on the Chesapeake with their own dock and sailboat behind the house. Elaine had visited them and Tommy took her out for a couple of days sailing on his 26-foot sailboat. Just once, and she was hooked! Sailing was all she could talk about. She repeatedly tried to convince me that I would love going five knots in a sailboat. To me, a good day on the water was seeing my jet boat above 80 mph and outrunning every other boat on the Ohio River. For a year she tried to talk me into chartering a sailboat in the Florida Keys with Tommy and Julia. I really thought it would be terribly boring, like watching grass grow. I finally gave in.

Tommy arranged for us to charter a 33-foot Watkins sloop from Treasure Harbor Charters on Tavernier Key. I went to the library and checked out a couple of "how to sail" books. I read the two books and told Elaine I was ready. I wasn't about to go sailing and not know a little something. Uncle Tommy called and we talked about what to take: navigational tools, foul weather gear, etc. He said we should pack our things in a duffel bag because there is no place to store hard luggage on a sailboat. I asked him why we would need navigational tools, we weren't getting out of sight of land, were we? He laughed. I spoke up and told Tommy I had read two books on sailing. He laughed louder. He asked me if I had practiced my knots, if I could cleat a dockline or do a clove hitch or a bowline. I told him I hadn't really gone to the trouble to get a piece of rope yet, but I had looked at the pictures. He asked if I knew the three rules for the right of way of sailboats. I just sat there. He asked me several questions I couldn't answer. He finally said that he had sailed for forty years and he probably only knew about 10% of what there is to know. I thought to myself, 10% in forty years, Uncle Tommy must not be too quick of a learner. He said not to worry too much about it, that I would learn a lot the week we were on the boat. It would take me a few years and several thousand miles of sailing before I would truly appreciate the significance of Uncle Tommy's 10%.

We arrived at Treasure Harbor all excited about our week in the Keys. While the women and Jason (our 13 year old at the time) put the luggage and supplies away on the boat, the charter owner went over the tide and the navigational charts with Tommy and I. I sure hoped Tommy knew what he was talking about because I was lost. The Keys are mostly shallow with a lot of coral heads and it's easy to run aground and damage the boat. The charter guy gave us these complex directions to get safely out to Hawk's Channel. I don't remember the exact figures but it went something like this. He told us to keep the first few markers close to starboard and, as we make the turn to port, stay close to the port markers. Once past the last marker, take a heading of such and such until we get to this point on the chart. You know you are at this point when this building is such and such degrees and this tower is this many degrees. Then go exactly a quarter of a mile at this heading until the building is this many degrees and the tower is this many degrees. Then take this heading and so on and so forth. He said we only had about a 40-minute window at high tide to get out of the harbor and through their channel and that high tide was in 30 minutes so we had better hurry. This guy looked at me and asked if we had any questions. I said, "This is a heck of a place to navigate out of but I think Tommy and I can handle it, can't we Tommy?" Tommy had been writing down all these figures. He didn't even look up when he asked the guy what channel on the VHF they monitor so we can call if we run aground. This guy told us a charter captain who had chartered boats for 16 years in the Keys ran aground the week before. Said he did a lot of damage all because of one wrong reading on the hand-held compass. Said we really need to stay on our toes. Uncle Tommy had almost a full page of scribbling --and that was only just to get out of the place. I was beginning to wonder if Uncle Tommy's 10% would be enough.

We successfully made all the right turns at all the right places and made it out to Hawk's Channel. Hawk's Channel is the main channel marked by buoys that small boats use to navigate through the Keys. We rubbed ground a few times, and I thought we were stuck one time for the rest of the night. Uncle Tommy pushed the throttle wide open, and we broke loose. We continued on at a very slow pace so, if we did hit something with the keel, it wouldn't hurt the boat too badly. I was beginning to wish I had studied the navigational techniques in those two sailing books.

We had just enough daylight to get to Long Key where I received my first lesson on anchoring. I told Elaine that night there may be more to this sailing than I thought. We had soup and sandwiches for supper and made our plans for the next day. There was a cold front in the Keys so we went to bed early to stay warm. The next day we would raise the sails. I lay there trying to remember everything I had memorized about the points of sail and thinking about what I had learned that day.

The next morning we listened to the weather station on the VHF, and it looked like we picked a bad week for cruising. They predicted rain and high winds from the west for at least three days. I wasn't going to let a little bad weather dampen my spirits. I was ready to learn about sailing. The next few days I would learn how to clean through-hull fittings, repair temperamental heads, change fuel filters and bleed a fuel system, clean a raw water strainer, unfoul anchor rodes, figure out battery banks, light an alcohol stove without burning the boat up, shower with a quart of water, and much, much more.

We stayed the next night at Bonefish Harbor on Fat Deer Key. I learned about docking sailboats. I learned that because of their single engine, sailboats do not maneuver very well. I also learned to anticipate the affect of the wind and current, and to have a game plan before attempting to dock.

The next day we motorsailed into 25 knot winds to get to Duck Key. We tied up at another marina because there wasn't any place to anchor. Duck Key was beautiful. Elaine and I went for a long walk, then we had a great dinner at the restaurant in the marina. I was really liking this sailboat thing and we hadn't really sailed yet. Tommy said we might just stay at Duck Key for a couple of days if the weather didn't improve. I told everyone that I really wanted to go to Marathon because I heard it would have hundreds of sailboats there. The marina at Duck Key only had fishing boats and cabin cruisers docked there. I wanted to see some sailboats. Besides that, we needed a lot of groceries and Marathon would be a good place to stock up.

The weather looked bad the next morning. The temperature dropped into the fifty's and the winds were 30 knots from the west. Tommy said Marathon was only about 5 miles west of us but it was going to be a rough ride. I said I could stand on my head for 5 miles. That is just about what I had to do. It took us about 2 hours to get half way there and then the engine alarm went off. The engine was running hot. I found a water pump impeller and went to work, standing on my head. By the time I changed the raw water impeller, we had drifted back to Duck Key. We started motorsailing again towards Marathon. The alarm went off again. Tommy said the through hull was probably stopped up with seaweed. I pulled up the floor boards and got to the through hull valve for the raw water. I pulled off the hose and opened the valve and no water came in. I took a clothes hanger and poked it down through the valve until water gushed in and soaked me before I could get the valve shut off. I put the hose back on and tightened the clamps. We started the engine. This time water was coming out the exhaust like it was suppose to. After five grueling hours, we finally made it to Marathon.

We motored through a little creek that had mangroves on the port side and houses on the starboard side. Tommy went down below to take some medicine and left me in charge. The little diesel was just chugging along and the wheel felt great in my hands. It was really relaxing puttering along at five knots and enjoying the view. Just being on the water has always been a rewarding experience to me. The waterway forked a couple of times as it snaked back through to Marathon Bay. I was so involved in the scenery that I made a wrong turn before I knew it. The waterway got narrower and narrower and there was no way to turn around. Everybody else was down below staying warm and I wasn't about to tell them I was lost. Finally there was a narrow waterway going to the right. I had to try to turn around here. The depth indicator was showing 5 and 6 feet and our draft was only 4 feet so I thought we could make it. Just as the bow got up between the mangroves, the keel hit sand and we came to a dead stop. I pulled it in reverse and gave it a little gas and it just sat there. Uncle Tommy came up in the cockpit along with everybody else. He looked around and could see nothing but mangroves. He asked what the depth was showing. I said 3 feet. He said a boat with 4 feet draft does not do well in 3 feet of water. I told him it was showing at least 5 feet when I tried to turn around. He knew better than to ask how we got in this mess. He knew I was lost. I felt like a real dunce. My first time behind the wheel of a sailboat and I ran it aground.

Tommy said that we were at high tide and, if we didn't get off now, we were stuck for the night. He told me to turn it hard to port and give it full throttle in reverse. If that didn't work, we would have to kedge our way out with the anchor. I remember reading about that kedging thing. Anyway, the boat just sat there for the longest time and I was really feeling down. Finally, it started creeping back just a little. It stopped again. Then it moved a little more. It started turning to port as we inched backwards. As soon as the bow cleared the mangroves I put it in forward and we were moving again. For the next 20 minutes there were five of us in the cockpit. No one said anything but it was obvious they wanted to make sure I didn't make any more wrong turns.

We motored into the bay and there right in front of us, were hundreds of sailboats at anchor. It was a phenomenal sight. Tommy took the wheel and said we would try to find a place to anchor close to the east end of the bay near the dingy dock and the shopping centers. I went to the bow and prepared the anchors. The wind was at least 30 knots from the west. It was definitely a two-anchor night. Since the dingy on this charter boat only had oars, we had to try to anchor close to the dingy dock to give me a chance to row back. And the only way we were going to eat supper that night was for me to dingy in and get some groceries.

We worked for at least an hour trying to get the anchors set. When they did set, Tommy thought we were too close to other boats. I bet I pulled those anchors up at least five times by hand. Finally we found a spot at least a half mile from the dingy dock where the anchors really grabbed and we were swinging clear of other boats. Tommy said this was the best we could do.

We went down below and had a cup of hot chocolate while the women made a grocery list. I put on Tommy's foul weather gear. We lowered the dingy from the forward deck. I climbed down and Tommy handed me the oars. There was some concern about me being able to row back into the wind and waves. I told them I owned a health club and rowed on a rowing machine several times a week. I would learn this day the difference between pulling on a handle seated on a rowing machine and pulling on a set of oars in a dingy trying to make headway into 30-knot winds and white capping seas.

It only took a few minutes to get to the dingy dock with the help of the wind. I tied the dingy up and walked the half mile to the grocery. I was feeling special. I was sacrificing the warmth and comfort of the boat to go and get food for the clan. I would be the hero before the day was over. I needed to do something special to make up for getting us stuck in the mangroves.

I went a little overboard. I had to carry back six full bags of groceries. By the time I got to the dingy dock my back was killing me and my arms were paralyzed. It was late in the afternoon and the bar at the dingy dock was full of sailors taking advantage of happy hour. I put the bags in the dingy and went back inside the bar for a brew to give me strength to row. I bellied up to the bar between two old "salts" and tried to strike up a conversation without any luck. I even bought them a round and still couldn't get them to talk. Buying them a beer will end up being one of the smartest things I've ever done. After two quick ones my back and arms started feeling better.

It was time to test my rowing abilities. I pushed the dingy out from the dock, into the wind and waves, and started rowing. I was rowing as hard and fast as I could but the wind and waves were overpowering. The dingy was going backwards. Instead of gaining ground, it lost ground. I finally gave up and grabbed a stern ladder on a sailboat anchored east of the bar. I had to rest for a while. It was obvious there was no way I could row into these conditions. I sat there hanging on to that ladder for about ten minutes trying to figure out how I was going to get out of this predicament. Finally, one of the old "salts" who I had bought a beer for came out of the bar, looked my way, and shook his head. I didn't know if I was hanging on to his boat or what. He got in an old wood-planked dingy with an antique little outboard that sounded like a model airplane engine and headed my way. He went past me and turned and came back by and tossed me a line. I grabbed hold and set back and braced myself. We went back by in front of the bar with everyone watching. It was embarrassing with all these experienced sailors getting a kick out of seeing this greenhorn being towed back to his boat.

The plan was for him to take me in front of the boat a ways and then I would let loose and coast back. I quietly worked my way back to the stern. I hollered, "Ahoy there mates, anybody hungry." Everyone came up in the cockpit and gave me a heroes' welcome. I started handing up groceries. They were going through the bags right there in the cockpit. They acted like they were starved. I told them it was one heck of a row. Tommy just shook his head--he couldn't believe it.

Dinner that night rates right up there as one of the best ever; ham fried in a skillet, potatoes and green beans out of a can, applesauce and fresh bread. Evidently, we were real hungry. I told Uncle Tommy after dinner that, if it's the last thing I do, I will become a good sailor. He kind of laughed and said I had a lot to learn, that it took years and years of experience to be a good sailor. Uncle Tommy didn't know how I did things. I told Tommy the whole story of how I got into motorcycle racing.

Two other couples and Elaine and I rented a pop-up trailer that slept six in March of 1969 and went to Daytona for a week of sun and fun. I had read about Daytona Motorcycle Week before but had no idea that we were going during motorcycle week. We were the only people in the campgrounds that weren't racing motorcycles of some type: flat-track, road race, enduro, or motorcross. One night there was a flat-track race inside the football stadium (the Daytona Short Track) and I talked the others into going. There were bikes sideways up in the corner handlebar to handlebar with the rear wheels squirting rooster tails of sand and limestone. I couldn't believe how they were laying the bikes over going into the corners and how fast they were going down the straights inside this football stadium. Over 200 riders went through qualifying heats, scratch heats, and semi's to eliminate down to the fastest twelve for the main event. The main event was the most exciting thing I had ever seen. These guys were modern-day gladiators. The hair stood straight up on my arms for days.

As we were leaving the stadium, I told the other two couples and Elaine that I would be out there the next year racing with those guys. They all laughed. They didn't believe me but I was there the next year and I was pretty fast. I usually did pretty good if I didn't crash. I was 25 years old when I started racing and I was the oldest rider to ever make enough points to make expert in two years. I did this while working full time as an aerospace engineer for Boeing on the Saturn/Apollo Missions. I told Tommy I won short track races and half mile races on dirt and indoors on concrete. I'm not sure he believed me but I wanted him to know that if I said I was going to do something, I would do it.

We stayed one more day at Marathon and I took lots and lots of pictures of sailboats. There were sailboats of every shape, size and sail plan. I planned on researching the facts on several of them when I got back to Owensboro. The next day we motored back out to Hawk's Channel. I suggested we "put a bone in her teeth" and sail back to Tavernier Key in one day. Uncle Tommy liked hearing that old saying, so we raised all the sail we had and did some serious down wind sailing. One week on a ragged old charter sailboat and I was hooked. The "sailing bug" had bitten me pretty hard and left me with an unexplainable disorder--so that I couldn't do anything without thinking about sailing. I couldn't work and I couldn't concentrate on pool or golf anymore. I didn't even want to go to professional motorcycle races anymore. When somebody talked to me about something I always answered with some comment about sailing. Close friends and family expressed concern, most of them thought I had lost it. I just wanted to go sailing.

Chapter 2

The day we bought Jaibolero

We bought Jaibolero, our Offshore 40 sailboat, on November 8, 1992. Everyone who has ever been bitten by the "sailing bug" has dreamed of the day that they will purchase their own sailboat--believing that day will be one of joy and satisfaction. We remember this day as a lot of "not-so-bad" happenings that all added up to one terrible, life-threatening situation. Believe me, the participants of this transaction will remember this day for the rest of their lives. I still get a "sick" feeling in my gut when I think about it. I have been known to embellish the truth a little but this story is one that I usually "tone down" trying to make it more believable.

Elaine and I have a good relationship that works for us, most of the time. She pretty much trusts my judgement and gives me free rein to do what I think is best, most of the time. However, she is kind of like the President in that she has veto power. If one of my proposals is too far out, then it is vetoed. I rarely ever have been able to override a veto. Elaine was fourteen years old when we started dating. The first day I met her, I went home and told my mother I had met the girl I was going to marry. The very next day I found out that she was interested in my friend and not me. But I didn't give up and we started dating a few weeks later. We were married when she was seventeen and I was nineteen. Our relationship has mostly revolved around my work or my hobbies. I didn't necessarily want it that way, but that's just the way things happened. Elaine always worked but, when it came time for me to change jobs and move, we did. My work carried more leverage. It was understood that I was the main provider and she liked it that way. She even went along with my hobbies, some of which were extreme. She helped me run the businesses, but I was the one who felt totally responsible for their failure or success. I was the one who suffered the sleepless nights and the days of agonizing indecision. I was the one who feared failure to the point of being obsessed. Elaine's two main worries were what we were having for supper and if the boys' new school clothes would get them the "best dressed" titles. This is the way things were for us and it worked. Nobody complained.

Buying a boat is a lot like getting a wife. There are a lot of fantastic looking boats out there but a person has to stay within their budget. Sometimes that fantastic looking boat sails like a slug. And almost always a real fancy boat requires a lot of maintenance. A neat, trim, low- maintenance sailboat that performed well was all I wanted. The thought of owning the boat of my dreams dominated my conscious mind for several months. The burden of finding that boat was on my shoulders as expected. I could wait no longer. After hundreds of long distance phone calls to owners and brokers all over the country, I located several boats up east, around Annapolis and on the Chesapeake Bay. We bought a new Chevy extended-cab pickup and took off for the boat show at Annapolis. We looked at hundreds of boats during the next four days but could not find that perfect boat in our price range. We headed back to Kentucky. The next day we left for Texas, New Orleans and the Gulf Coast. My dream boat was somewhere and we were going to find it. We stopped at every marina from New Orleans to Panama City. We looked at boat after boat after boat. Elaine was getting tired and frustrated. I took her back to Kentucky and dropped her off, then drove straight through to Miami to look at some more boats. The sticker on my windshield showed it was time to change the oil again. It had been changed just five days earlier. The truck had been 6000 miles in ten days. I called home and Elaine was worried about me. She said, "Your excessive compulsive behavior disorder is maxed out." I didn't care. I knew I wasn't crazy. There wasn't anything wrong with me that the right boat wouldn't cure. I just had to find it.

After Miami I drove to Tampa and then down to Ft. Myers and back over to Melbourne and Jacksonville and then back to Daytona. It was almost giving-up time. I called Elaine and told her it was time for me to head home. There were several boats that were interesting, but none were really that perfect boat. Elaine guessed we had set our goals too high.

On the way back to the motel after eating, I stopped at a little marina that had a few sailboats. A broker was there checking out a small sailboat that he was listing. I told him what I was looking for and followed him back to his office. While he was out, Charlie Morgan's office in Tampa had faxed him a spec sheet on a boat that sounded interesting. I went back to the motel, checked out, and drove to Tampa so I could be there when they opened up in the morning. I pulled into the parking lot for the downtown marina, which was close to Charlie Morgan's office, and got a couple hours sleep before the sun came up. It was Friday morning and the lady at the desk said she did not know anything about the boat in question and everyone else was at a boat show. She said someone should check in before noon and she would ask them about the boat. She told me to check back later. There wasn't anything to do but wait for the call. To pass the time, I started looking through the photo books of boats they had listed and sold through the years.

About eleven o'clock the UPS driver dropped off a large padded envelope. The secretary opened it and made a comment that somebody sure went to a lot of trouble and expense to sell a used boat. She handed me the brochure. It was phenomenal. There were about a dozen pages with professional photos and illustrations. There was not a question anyone could ask about the boat that was not answered in

Jaibolero in Panama City at Bay Point Marina

the brochure. It even had pictures of the boat at different stages of construction. I could not believe my eyes. It was exactly what I was looking for.

This was my dream boat and I had to see it. The secretary told me to come back next week and talk with one of the brokers to see the boat. She had no earthly idea what this meant to me. I told her that I had to see the boat that day and that it was a matter of life and death. She looked at me with concern. I said I had driven over 7000 miles in two weeks looking at boats and that I would probably die if I had to wait a week to see it. She recognized the affliction that had come over me for she evidently had seen other sailboat crazy people who had been bitten by the same bug. I didn't care. I offered to write her a check for ten percent of the listing price and said I had no intentions of beating them out of their commission. She tried to ignore me for a while but I just stood there in front of her. She finally felt sorry for me and called the owner. She said it was against their rules, that she would probably get fired, but she didn't want to have my life on her conscience. She put me on the phone with the owner. He agreed to show me the boat and gave me the directions. He said it would take me five hours if I didn't stop to eat. I said I would be there in less than four--and I was.

Jaibolero was at Shell Point, Florida, just a few miles south of Tallahassee. He was in the water at a private dock behind the owner's house. That song, "just one look, that's all it took," flashed through my mind. This was definitely my dream boat. It was custom built by Nautical Development and designed by the Cruising World Design Team to be the ultimate cruiser for a couple. It was a 40-foot center

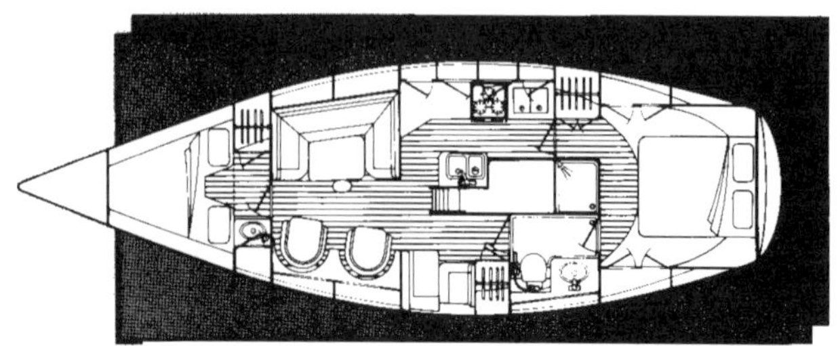

Floor plan of an Offshore 40 by Nautical Development

cockpit with a great floor plan. It had a queen-size centerline aft birth, V-berth forward, separate shower, great nav station, large galley with lots of storage, salon with beveled glass mirrors, roller-furling on all three sails, custom dingy davits, 25 gallons per hour water maker, etc.

It was love at first sight. It didn't take me ten seconds to know I had to have this boat. The owner was a fanatic. No one ever stepped on the boat except with bare feet. Ten coats of varnish on the teak and holly floor. Eight years old and the shower had never been used. They would shower on deck so the one down below would not get messed up. No water was ever left standing in the head. It looked like it had never been used. It was porcelain white even in the very bottom. The boat was aired out almost every day. It showed no signs of salt or corrosion. Pictures usually flattered the boats we had looked at. Jaibolero was better than the pictures. Most sailboats are referred to as a her or she, like in female. Jaibolero just did not sound like a girl's name. For this reason I always refer to Jaibolero as a he or him. We were to find out later that Jaibolero was a Spanish slang word for "keep on trucking."

It was hard trying to be "cool" and act like he was just another sailboat. My knees were getting weak. I suggested that we sit down and talk. I told the gentleman that I wasn't one to beat around the bush, that I was going to make him an offer. Now it was his turn to play it cool and beat around the bush, he ignored my offer. I just sat there waiting for a response. Finally, he told me it was a fair offer but that he had to sleep on it. He had no idea what he was doing to me. This was Friday afternoon and he asked me to call him Monday morning at 9 AM. He would let me know then if he would sell it. I tried pulling a bluff and said, if he couldn't let me know now, then I wasn't interested. He said he would not talk to anyone else about the boat or show it to anyone over the weekend. He just did not know if he wanted to sell it at any price. I couldn't have felt worse if he had run over me with a steam roller. There was nothing I could do but drive back to Kentucky and wait. I did call Charlie Morgan's office the next morning and told the lady not to tell anyone else about Jaibolero until after Monday because I thought I had it bought.

It was a long weekend. I called Monday morning--and he said he was probably going to regret it, but he would sell me the boat. Words could not describe my elation. We arranged for a closing date on the first Sunday in November.

To keep from paying sales tax, we had to get Jaibolero out of the state within 30 days. Our plan was to sail him over to Mobile, keep him there for the required six months, and then bring him back to Panama City. With good weather it would take about six days of day sailing to get to Mobile. We drove to Mobile and rented a car. We transferred everything over to the car and headed for Shell Point. This way our truck would be waiting for us at Turner's Marine in Mobile when we got there. We arrived at Jaibolero on Sunday morning so the owner could go over all of the equipment before the sea trial.

With Jaibolero's draft of 5'3", there is only about a 30-minute window at high tide in which we could motor out through the channel for a test sail. Once we were out, Jaibolero had to stay out for the night. High tide was at 2:40 that afternoon and we rubbed bottom a couple of times getting out. The wind had picked up to 20-25 knots from the NE. The owner told us that after the test sail we would have to anchor out in the open bay and dingy everyone back to shore and do the paperwork. Then Elaine and I could dingy back out and we would get to spend the night on Jaibolero. Sounds simple. Well, it wasn't.

The seas were from four to six feet by the time we lowered the dingy in the water and put the 5 horsepower Sears Gamefisher motor on it. It was after 4 PM and the temperature had already dropped into the thirties. It also started misting rain. We had anchored at the end of the locally-maintained channel that extends at least a mile out into Apalachee Bay. The broker weighed nearly 300 pounds--so it was going to take two trips to get all five of us to shore. It was the owner, the broker and I on the first trip. We only had one rain suit so I left it for Elaine. With the broker sitting up front, the poor dingy was half sunk to start with and it didn't take long for the breaking waves to fill it half full of water. We were taking the waves off the starboard bow and we were going so slow at times that I thought we were backing up. The waves were very close together and steep because the water was so shallow. We could hardly make it over the waves. There was a restaurant on shore and the game plan was to do the closing there. We had been fighting these waves for what seemed like an hour and we were still a long way from shore. We were soaked to the bone and freezing to death. If the engine quit, we were in big trouble. It would be impossible to row into the waves and make it to shore. The direction of the wind and waves would make it tough to row back to Jaibolero. It would take several hours of rowing to hit any land west of us. I doubted we would survive that long. Our lives depended on the little motor.

We were about 200 yards from shore when the motor hit bottom. I had to get out and walk the dingy the rest of the way to shore to let the others out. I turned around and headed back to Jaibolero. It had been dark for a while now and was still raining. I was so cold that I had a major case of the shakes. I could barely see the anchor light. Jaibolero looked like he was miles away. There is no describing how cold I was. The wind was blowing harder and the waves were getting bigger. It was insane to go back out to Jaibolero but I couldn't just leave the women out there all night. If the anchor broke loose or the equipment failed, they would be in real trouble. I could just imagine how upset Elaine was and all this was definitely my fault. I talked to the little motor the whole way back, telling it how good a little motor it was, and that good little motors don't quit at a time like this. If it quit, I knew I would die from exposure before morning. It was time for a serious discussion with the Lord. I told Him that if He would help us get out of this mess, I would never do anything this stupid again. I thought about all the crazy things I had done in my life and survived--now my life depended on this $200 little outboard.

When I finally made it back out to Jaibolero, his stern was going up and down about ten feet with every wave and it didn't look like the ladies were going to be able to get in the dingy. How in the world did we ever get in this predicament? Finally, I made a pass by the ladder and the owner's wife jumped in the dingy. Now, it was Elaine's turn. Elaine cannot swim. She did not know what to do. I told her she had to go sign the papers or we couldn't close the deal. She did not want to jump in the dingy. She was terrified. I pleaded and begged and she finally agreed to give it a try. If the dingy got too close, the ladder could come down and rip it apart. I made another close pass and Elaine jumped. She landed in the dingy but the momentum was taking her over the opposite side. I grabbed her jacket and barely kept her in the dingy. It wasn't funny but I couldn't help laughing.

This reminded me of the time I took Elaine to meet my parents and go horseback riding. I was sixteen and she was fourteen. My family has always had horses. It was a Sunday afternoon and the whole family and some other friends were there. It was Elaine's turn to show us her riding skill. I showed her how to hold the reins, put her left foot in the stirrup, grab a hold of the saddlehorn and pull herself up in the saddle. She really wanted to impress my parents. She pulled herself up and over and landed on her bottom on the other side. It was hysterical. Everyone was laughing. I went around the horse to help her up and she pushed my hand away. She had these big tears in her eyes. She wasn't hurt, just terribly embarrassed. I really felt sorry for her but I couldn't stop laughing. It was months before she would go back to my parent's house.

By the time we made it to shore, I think the hypothermia had me incoherent. I was singing "row, row, row your boat" and laughing and having a good time. It really wasn't cold anymore. I was past that point. It was about 7 PM when I pulled the dingy ashore and let the ladies out. We went inside and ordered buckets of coffee. We signed the papers and gave them the wet but readable cashier's check. Everyone was anxious to get out of their wet clothes so the closing didn't take long. Elaine and I headed for the dingy for our much-dreaded trip back out to Jaibolero. I thought I would have a hell of time getting her back in the dingy, but she just climbed right in without any argument. She must have been in a state of shock. The weather had become even worse with 25-30 knot winds and huge breaking waves. It was hard to judge the height of the waves, especially at night in total darkness, but they had to be eight to ten feet high and breaking. Our Avon rib was a pretty stable little dingy but, with these seas conditions, we were going to be lucky to keep it right side up. On the way back out to Jaibolero, the little engine started missing. I told Elaine I hoped she was praying because, if this little engine quits, we are done for and the next stop would be Mexico. I didn't know until a couple of days later but there wasn't a thimble of gas left in the tank when we got back to the boat. It was running on fumes. I had nightmares about this for months. Floating out in the Gulf in a dingy for days with Elaine, her not saying anything, and no food and water. Sharks swimming everywhere. Its a miracle we were alive.

We made it back to Jaibolero and the next challenge was to get safely back on board. The stern ladder was way up out of the water one instant and way down in the water the next instant. It was going to take an acrobatic act to grab the ladder and get on board. Elaine never ceased to amaze me. When it comes to saving her life she can get pretty tough. She can't swim a lick, is no "spring chicken," and has rheumatoid arthritis. I maneuvered the dingy close to the ladder and Elaine grabbed it and climbed up it like she was a teenager.

Our first day on Jaibolero was suppose to be great. For weeks we had dreamed about how wonderful our first night anchoring out would be. This dream turned into a nightmare. It was not my fault that everything turned out wrong. I had no idea that we could not get Jaibolero back to the dock after a test sail or that we would have to anchor out so far and dingy everyone back to shore in these terrible conditions. I did not know that the broker, for liability reasons, would insist that we take a test sail. There is no way anyone could make up a more horrible set of conditions. No amount of explaining to Elaine could make things better. It was all my fault, and I had to accept responsibility for the biggest screw-up of our lives.

We finally got into some warm, dry clothes. It would take hours for us to quit shaking. Elaine was awfully quiet. I hate it when she's this way. I knew I was in big trouble. This could be the end to our sailing and we hadn't even started yet. I tried to make things better. I told her I was kind of glad all of that had happened and that everything always turns out for the best. It was just one of those tests God puts people through to show them they are tougher than they think they are. It should make her feel good to know that we survived something like this. Now we've got something to tell the grandkids. She accused me of being insane. She didn't want our grandkids to think we were that stupid. In fact, she didn't want anyone to know about this, ever. I stated that the good times were in front of us, that nothing could be much worse than what we had just gone through today. She accused me of jinxing us for sure. She said, if she had any sense whatsoever, she would jump ship the first chance she got and leave this insanity to me because things were probably going to get a lot worse if I had anything to do with it. I hate to admit it but she was right. This day was nothing in comparison to what happened just three days later.

Chapter 3

The good, the bad, and the ugly.

We did not sleep the first night we stayed on Jaibolero. We only put out one anchor because we were told there was good holding at the end of the channel off Shell Point. I was told to put out plenty of anchor rode and I did. I don't know about other sailboats, but Jaibolero sure moves around a lot in high winds with only one anchor. He would not point into the wind. He swung back and forth through about 120 degrees all night long. He would take off to the left and pick up speed until the chain anchor rode would snatch him around to a port tack; then he would take off in a big arc in the other direction. At the end of the arc, the chain would yank him around and then he would be on a starboard tack heading in the opposite direction. He went back and forth all night long. This, plus a very hectic day, resulted in a restless night for both of us. It was cold and we didn't have heat, so we both put on several layers of clothes. We got under all the blankets and we were still cold. It was a long night. There was no way either of use could go to sleep. About 4:30 in the morning, the chain slipped on the windlass making a horrible noise. I got up to check it out and when I came back to bed Elaine asked, "Are we having fun yet?" I answered, "The first little thing goes wrong and you develop an attitude." We laid there the rest of the night waiting for the sun to come up so we could put up the sails and find a better anchorage for the next night.

As soon as there was some daylight we were sailing. We had at least 20 and up to 35-knot winds on our stern all day. The autopilot could not handle strong winds directly on its stern. Jaibolero was happier with winds about 30 degrees off his stern and there was less of a chance of an accidental jibe. This course would add a few miles, but the autopilot worked better at this point of sail. I finally laid down in the cockpit to rest. Jaibolero had "a bone in his teeth" and sailed well, as expected. We were doing more than maximum hull speed as we surfed off the top of waves. We saw ten knots a few times. This was really sailing. I was the happiest person on planet earth. Elaine was a little cautious. She wasn't really saying anything. It was normal to be cautious after all we had been through the day before. I knew that I needed to do something to make things better. If we could just have a good day of sailing with no surprises, she would have confidence in my sailing ability again.

Just before we broached. Am I content or what?

With the autopilot in control, Jaibolero was doing a great job sailing on a broad reach with 20-25 knot winds. I asked Elaine to watch things for a few minutes and I went sound asleep. All good things come to an end. A wind gust of at least 35 knots hit us and the autopilot lost control. We broached, rounded up broadside to the wind and sea, and the sails went in the water. A broach is caused by having too much sail up in steep seas and, as the boat is just past the crest with the bow down, the rudder loses its effectiveness. This can be very dangerous if the boat rolls over. The broach was a rude awakening. I jumped behind the wheel, kicked the autopilot off, and pointed him back down wind so that the headsail was covered by the main. I did not know if the winds were going to get worse or not. I could tell by the look on

Elaine's face that I had to do something quick--and it had better be right. I had to get the headsail in. We were on a starboard tack so I had to step outside the cockpit on the leeward side to roll in the headsail. I don't think I was fully awake yet. I told Elaine to release the headsail sheets and she did, all of them. She should have kept a double wrap on the winch and let the sheet out until the headsail luffed. The headsail sheets are stored in covered compartments next to the winches in the cockpit. I did not check to see if the sheets had stop knots to prevent them from flying loose.

I will try to explain what happens when over 100 feet of 9/16 inch ropes, called headsail sheets, get loose in 30 to 35-knot winds. They become dangerous weapons. The headsail is flying loose in the wind and headsheets become huge deadly whips. The loose ends start to tie in knots and they start growing as they are whipped in the wind. They keep getting bigger. The bigger the knots, the more dangerous they become.

I was outside the cockpit on the port side pulling on the roller furling line trying to roll in the headsail and making very little progress and these headsheets with knots were trying to beat me to death. If one of the headsheets had wrapped around my neck, it would have snapped it like a match stick. One knot hit me on the shoulder and one hit me squarely in the middle of my back. If one smacked me up beside the head and I went overboard, I was in one hell of a fix. Elaine and I had not worked on the man-overboard drill yet. In fact, about the only thing Elaine knows how to do on the boat was cook. I doubt if she could physically release the mainsail because of her arthritis, turn Jaibolero around, and pick me up in these conditions. I wasn't real sure she would come back and get me if she could. I wasn't real sure she wasn't going to kill me if we lived through this mess. I decided discretion is the better part of valor. I wanted to live to sail another day. I had one choice, and that was to give up trying to roll in the headsail. I jumped back into the cockpit behind the dodger for protection. Elaine looked worried. She asked me what I was supposed to do now. I didn't know. I just sat there and watched these knots grow as the headsail whipped back and forth. In a few minutes the knots ended up being about two feet in diameter at the clew of the headsail. We sailed for about thirty minutes with the headsail flying free with these two huge balls of knotted-up rope dangerously whipping back and forth. They were hitting the shrouds with such force that I thought the whole rig was going to come down at any minute. Then, the winds finally slacked off a little and I finally was able to roll in the headsail. It was going to need restitching and new sun protection material, but it wasn't destroyed.

With the winds down to 20-25 knots again, I was able to unravel the big balls of sheets. I rerouted the sheets and tied stop knots to keep them from flying free. With about 50% of the headsail and the mainsail reefed down about one third, I set the autopilot again and Jaibolero was sailing along peacefully at 7 to 8 knots. Elaine was upset. I had too much sail up, and this was what had caused us to broach. I was pushing Jaibolero too hard, and she knew it. I tried to explain to her that you don't know where your limits are until you find them. In motorcycle racing, you don't know how fast you can go unless you crash. Then you know you went too fast. It was obvious that she was not in the mood for this logic. Elaine was wondering what would happen next. She was not talking. This was going to be our one and only trip on Jaibolero if things didn't get better quick. I bet there are people who have sailed for years and have never broached, and we broached on our first day out.

This made me think about the first day we were on a sailboat by ourselves. The summer after we first chartered with Uncle Tommy and Aunt Julia we decided to rent a Catalina 27 on Kentucky Lake for a few days around the end of July. I had to exaggerate a little about my sailing experience in order to convince the charter company that I could handle a sailboat. I think it was my gray hair and beard that did it. I looked like an old salt.

The first two days we would motor out to the middle of the lake and raise sails and wait for the wind to blow. There was no wind whatsoever, the sails just hung there. It was unbearably hot. We were swimming in our own sweat! Finally, on the third day, I gave up and went to the golf course. On about the tenth hole, clouds started covering the sky and the wind started moving the leaves on the trees. I told the two guys we were with that Elaine and I were going sailing. We rushed back to the marina as fast as we could and headed out toward the lake. Everyone else was coming in. Someone even yelled at us something about storm warnings as we left the dock. I thought, good, now we will have some wind. So what if it rains a little, Elaine can stay down below and I sure wasn't going to melt. Elaine expressed some concern. I told her we were on an ocean-going sailboat and it could easily handle a little storm on Kentucky Lake.

Elaine took the wheel while I put up the full mainsail and rolled out the headsail. I knew I should have reefed the mainsail but I hadn't figured out how to do that, yet. We were going south in about 20 mph winds from the west. We were a little overpowered, a little too much sail up, but we were going fast. We had the whole lake to ourselves. Elaine went down below. I was thinking to myself that those other sailboats don't know what they're missing. Then, all of a sudden, bang, the mast and sails were in the water and I almost went overboard. I was hanging on to the life lines. I climbed back in the cockpit and was standing on the back of the seat on the port side. A powerful gust of wind had knocked us over. We took a knockdown on Kentucky Lake. The wind blew like crazy for several minutes. Elaine yelled up from the main cabin and asked, "What in the devil are you doing?" I told her, "I don't know." She commented, "That's lovely, are we sinking?" I told her, "I don't think so."

The boat turned into the wind and started coming back up like it was suppose to do and I released the headsail sheets. The wind slacked off and I rolled in about half of the headsail and turned off the wind and we were sailing again. Elaine stuck her head up in the hatchway and had that "deer-in-the-headlight" look. I told her a strong gust of wind blew us over but her multi-talented husband had saved the day and we were sailing again. She said we were sinking and that water was above the floorboards. I turned the bilge pump on and the water started going down. The water was really nasty. We had taken some water through an open port but most of it came from the holding tank. Somehow the holding tank dumped back through the head. Elaine's purse had fallen off a shelf and dumped everything in it in sewage water. Boy, she was some kind of mad. She was never going out in a boat with me again. Needless to say, I had the job of cleaning up the mess when we got back to the dock. That night, at the restaurant, people were saying that the airport reported gusts of 72 mph.

I had done it again. Our first day on our own sailboat out in Apalachee Bay and we broached. We sailed a couple of more hours with neither one of us saying anything. We found a good anchorage with wind and wave protection for the night. It felt good to be safe. I also felt a sense of accomplishment--we had survived a real precarious situation and I had learned a valuable lesson.

The confidence a sailor acquires when a good landfall is made after a rough passage is part of what sailing is all about. A big part of the spice that a threat of danger lends keeps sailing exciting. We had our first supper on Jaibolero. It was great. We were both exhausted and went to bed early. I lay there for hours thinking about the seriousness of the headsheet incident. Wondering how many things can go wrong on a sailboat and how ill prepared we really were. Our first day of sailing on our dream boat had some good sailing, a bad broach and an ugly incident when the headsheets were loose.

The next morning we were having breakfast and Elaine suggested that we just stay where we were for a day or so. She felt that we would be safe and nothing bad was likely to happen to us in this anchorage. She told me I needed to read my "how to sail" books again. I told her she really knew how to kill a man's confidence. I had heard about people who would have a bad experience sailing and get "port sickness." They would stay in one spot for months and sometimes, years, so they wouldn't have to go out and sail again. They must have had some pretty bad experiences. It looked like Elaine was about to get a case of "port sickness." I told her that we were doing pretty good. Jaibolero was still floating, we were alive and that we had learned a lot. Before this trip was over I was going to be one smart sailor. All I had to do was learn from my mistakes. I had made enough of them. The look on her face showed that she did not appreciate the humor.

After a little persuading I convinced her that we should go on. We raised anchor and had an uneventful sail to Panama City. One whole day of sailing and no near catastrophes. We had a record going. One day with no surprises. Elaine told me that's probably all it would be, just a one-day record. She didn't realize it, but she jinxed us for sure this time. We tied up at Passport Marine on the Big Lagoon. Elaine and I went to Captain Anderson's to eat and things were looking up.

She started to talk again and smiled every once in awhile. Good food works wonders with her.

While on a walk after dinner, we talked about looking forward to the day we could take off on Jaibolero for a long, extended cruise. I probably did most of the talking. One thing for sure about Elaine, she loves to travel. Back in the motorcycle racing days, every time the van was loaded and ready to go, she too was ready to go. She's probably part Gypsy. I knew how to get her in a better mood. We talked about the secluded beaches and anchorages, the islands to explore and the sights to see. We talked about the wonderful relaxing crossings in the steady trade winds and about the new friends we would make. The gleam came back in her eyes.

Our son Jason had two more years of high school and then we were "gone." We had to sell our home and get a smaller one. We also had two more businesses to sell with long-term leases on the properties and improvements. I had already sold two others and leased the real estate. We had a Morgan 32 on Kentucky Lake for the last couple years. It had to be sold. A lot of things had to fall into place before we could leave. If there was a will, there was a way. I loved my boat and I was going cruising sometime in the near future.

Elaine reminded me that we hadn't made it to Mobile yet. I told her I could swim to Mobile from Panama City. That we had a forty foot sailboat designed to handle just about everything the sea could dish out and we only had about 85 more miles of sailing in the Gulf. Two day sails: one for 45 miles to Destin and another 40 miles to Pensacola. After that we would motor the intercoastal over to Mobile. I tried to convince her it would be a "piece of cake." Elaine wanted to believe me but the look on her face expressed concern.

Chapter 4

Tiger by the tail.

The next morning was November 11, 1992. We had slept like babies. Our queen-size berth was the most comfortable bed I had ever slept in. I woke up feeling rested and ready to grab the tiger by the tail. Little did I know I really would before the day was over. Before we continued on our mission to get Jaibolero to Mobile, I needed to replace the headsail furling sheet because it was frayed and stretched. I wanted to have him in as good a shape as possible. We didn't need any more surprises.

By the time I borrowed a truck and ran into town to get the line for fixing the roller furling, it was 10 AM. The weather station forecasted a front with high winds moving up from Texas that would hit the Ft. Walton and Destin area sometime after midnight. It was only about 40 miles to Destin, and I told Elaine we would be safely at anchor way before the storm got there. I don't know why she believed me, but she did. We cast off and headed for Destin.

The winds were around 20 knots from the NE. We were on a broad reach and making great time. Jaibolero was trucking along at 7+ knots. Sailing doesn't get any better than this. It could have been warmer but I didn't care. I told Elaine I would treat her at Harry T's that night. She smiled.

About 3 PM the sky started looking dark way off to the southwest. The Loran showed we were about 8 miles from the buoy marking the channel going into Destin. Elaine expressed concern. I told her we would be at anchor before the storm got to us. Wrong. About 3:30 the wind direction swung around to the southwest and the winds started picking up. How could the weatherman miss it this badly?

Elaine looked at me with disgust. She didn't have to say anything. I rolled in the headsail and the mainsail and put the staysail out. The staysail was my stormsail. Elaine went below for life jackets. She was getting pretty good at recognizing when we were in trouble.

I cranked the engine and motored. The winds were about 30 degrees off the port bow. The winds got stronger and stronger and the waves started busting over our bow. Jaibolero was pointing up at the sky one minute and almost straight down the next. The waves were bigger than I could ever imagine. The wind meter showed 50 knots and I couldn't hold him just off the wind. Before we knew it, we had blown over on our side. I pushed the throttle wide open and after a few tries was able to bring him back into the wind. Elaine took the wheel and I started rolling in the staysail. The wind was horrible and it looked like the rig was coming down before I could roll in the staysail. The rain was so heavy at times we couldn't see past the dodger. The sound of the rain hitting the dodger was horrible. The wind was screaming through the shrouds and making more horrifying sounds. I just knew the dodger and bimini were history. I was beginning to think we may be history.

People sail their whole lives and never see 40 knot winds. How could we have gotten caught out in this stuff? I guess I should have been scared, but I wasn't; I was too busy fighting for our lives. I tried to comfort Elaine and told her it would slack off any minute. Wrong again. Just as we thought things couldn't get worse, they did. We saw 60, 65, and 70-knot winds. I had the engine red-lined and was trying to keep Jaibolero pointed into the wind.

It was time to consider our options. We could turn around and put out some warps and head back to Panama City. Warps are long ropes that should slow us down and keep us from "pitch-poling" end over end off the steep waves. If the engine quit and the winds died down a little, we could put out the staysail and make it back. All the ports and hatches were closed. If we took a bad knockdown, we would stay afloat. I didn't want to think about a roll over, we didn't have any safety harnesses. They were on our want list. We had on good life jackets, and if the worst happened, we could get the life raft overboard and shore was not far away. The wind and waves were from a direction that would wash us ashore. Once we got to shore, I wasn't sure we could survive 20-foot waves slamming us onto the beach. Even if we didn't break our fool necks, we would probably drown. If Jaibolero did a 360 degree roll and we couldn't get to the life raft, we would have to swim for it. It was bad, real bad. Elaine was hanging on for dear life. I could tell this was the straw that broke the camel's back. Elaine would never sail again, and I wasn't so sure about me. Finally the winds eased up to about 50 knots. I told her if the boat goes over, swim for shore. She reminded me that she couldn't swim. I tried being funny and told her that she was crazier than me, out here in the ocean, in a sailboat and can't even swim. I reminded her that she was the one that got me into this, her and her Uncle Tommy, rest his soul. I'd be home playing golf if wasn't for her.

We decided to try to make it to Destin. With the engine wide open for over three hours, we were barely making headway against the wind and seas. We were still four miles from Destin. It was dark. I wasn't giving up. We were going to anchor in Destin harbor tonight. The wind had eased up to about 40 knots. Elaine went below to get on the radio and find out how the entrance was in these conditions. She raised somebody on the radio. There had to be several knowledgeable people listening on channel 16 and Elaine had to get the town fool. I still don't understand why somebody didn't break in and tell us this guy was going to get us killed. There are always other boaters listening to channel 16, especially in these conditions. This fool told Elaine he had sailed in and out of Destin for years and as long as we stayed in the channel we would make it across the sandbar with no trouble. My charts showed a shallow area about a half a mile offshore and the channel went right across it. The charts did not say that it was impassable in high offshore winds. I did not have the experience to know one way or the other.

I lined up the lights and headed in. It was raining and the seas were down to 10-15 feet. I was concentrating on the red and green lights and making sure that we stayed in the channel. There were so many other lights on shore that they were very easy to lose sight of if you didn't concentrate. My first time ever to enter a port at night and it had to be Destin and in these conditions. I started to suggest to Elaine that she could say a little prayer, that it couldn't hurt anything.

I didn't because she was already frightened enough.

The next thing we knew a wave passed us and we went down and hit bottom pretty hard. The next wave lifted the stern of Jaibolero up and the bow went down and stuck in the sand and he fell over on his starboard side. He was hard aground and abeam to the on coming waves. He would float upright a little and the next wave would crash over the top of us and knock him back down. Thank God it was sand instead of coral or rocks and thank God that Jaibolero is a well-built boat because he was in for one hell of a beating. We did not have safety harnesses, and I was worried that we would be washed out of the cockpit. I had to get him off this sandbar. As he would float up, I would push the throttle wide open and turn the wheel. If he would turn back into the waves, then we might be able to get him off. The rudder was stuck in the sand. I pulled on the wheel as hard as I could and as a wave floated us up, it finally broke loose. The next wave hit us, and he turned a little more into the waves. After a couple of more waves, he was pointing into the waves. With the throttle wide open, we bounced off the bottom eight or ten more times and finally broke free.

We motored back out to the buoy and just floated there for a few minutes, thinking. Elaine was quiet again. I had the shakes. I was mad, soaked to the bone, cold and scared. The dodger had kept Elaine fairly dry. I finally told her to get whoever she was talking to on the radio and tell him we ran aground following his stupid directions. She suggested that I talk to the idiot. I did. He said the sandbar was less than 100 yards wide and that it was shoaled up more on the left side. He said to stay lined up more on the red light, the right side of the channel. Maybe the guy was right. He did sound confident and we did not want to sail all night to get back to Panama City. I told Elaine what he had said, that we were going to try it again. She just sat there in a trance. I hate it when she's that quiet. I think she was numbed by all that had happened during the last three days.

We headed back in, slow and cautious. Not only was I watching the lights, I was watching the waves, too. As we approached the point where we got into trouble before, I could see the waves breaking. These waves looked like great surfing waves. For as far as we could see, it looked shallow all the way across in front of us. As we were turning around to go back out we brushed bottom again. We went back out to the buoy again and floated some more.

I had a game plan, but I wasn't about to tell Elaine. She would be convinced I was nuts. She asked me what we were going to do next. I told her I didn't know. I was watching the waves and timing them. Every fifth or sixth wave was a big one and the waves appeared to be going about 10-12 knots. Coming across Appalachee Bay, Jaibolero had surfed some big waves for a pretty good distance. The direction of the wind and waves and the channel heading going into Destin were basically the same. I turned him around and headed back in but, this time under full throttle. Maximum hull speed is eight knots and, if I could get Jaibolero on the front of the peak of a big wave and keep him there, I thought we could make it across safely. I experimented with a couple of big waves and by working the wheel a little to starboard, Jaibolero would stay on top of a wave for a pretty good distance. This sounds crazy, but I felt I could surf him across the sandbar. If we could just make it most of the way, the waves would eventually wash us the rest of the way across. We might lose some more bottom paint but we could still survive. I was just about to change my mind and turn around when I saw this big wave coming. I told Elaine to hold on, we were going surfing. Elaine accused me of being totally insane. I didn't have time to reply. I was in deep concentration--trying to save our lives. We were lucky and caught the wave just right. It was a spooky feeling, this 24,000 pound sailboat surfing on the top of a wave. I had to turn the wheel a little a couple of times when he felt like he might broach but I was able to keep him just on the front of the wave. The wave started to die down, and we were going to hit bottom. But we didn't. We were safely across. I told Elaine that nobody was going to believe this. She told me that she didn't even believe it.

We motored along a couple of minutes with neither one of us saying a word. I did my "thank you, Lord" in silence. I told Elaine that Jaibolero and I had saved the day, that we were a tough combination. She looked rather perturbed and said it was her and Jesus that got this boat across that sandbar, and I had nothing to do with it. It was her praying and Jesus's hands that lifted the boat up and set us down on the other side. I said I had to have something to do with it. She wouldn't give me any credit whatsoever. She's probably right. It definitely was some kind of a miracle.

We weren't out of the woods yet. We still had to negotiate the breakers and a channel full of buoys in the rain and strong winds. At the end of the channel is a bridge and just before it on the right is the very narrow and hard-to-see entrance to the harbor. Elaine went down below to get the spotlight. The new spotlight did not work. Couldn't just one thing go right? We had developed a wiring problem I didn't know about. I sent Elaine up to the bow with a handheld flashlight to try to spot the buoys. We had survived too much today to end up knocking a hole in Jaibolero's topsides with a buoy. We had just cleared the breakers and turned into the channel when a large green buoy missed our port side by about a foot. It was obvious the flashlight wasn't doing any good. I slowed Jaibolero down to a crawl. We had to try and feel our way in. If we were going slowly enough it wouldn't hurt too much if we hit something. We could not see the small markers to the entrance to the bay in these conditions until we were on top of them. This was not fun. If we ran aground to the right, we are stuck out in the channel for the night. If we got in trouble on the port side, there were the bridge abutments that would destroy Jaibolero in a matter of minutes. If we didn't keep our speed up, the wind would blow us into the bridge. I could tell by the chart approximately where the entrance was suppose to be, and we were going to have to go for it. Just when I thought I had made a big mistake, we saw the opening and turned inside and immediately dropped anchor. We were not suppose to anchor there, but this was as far as we were going. We were safe, for now. We were very lucky or we had a lot of help from up above: one or the other or probably both.

Chapter 5

Making Friends

The next morning was dreary and rainy. I was one happy sailor having survived the day before. Jaibolero had proved he was a well-founded, offshore sailboat. He took a lickin' and came back kickin'. Elaine cooked us breakfast. It was the best we'd ever eaten. Back home it would be just a regular breakfast but that morning on the boat, it was great. It's funny how invigorating mornings are on a boat. That, plus the pride of knowing we survived a great challenge, combined to make me feel like a million dollars. Elaine suggested that we get a slip in a marina for the night. We needed supplies and needed to do laundry. The thought entered my mind that she might take off running and never look back if she ever got her feet on solid ground again. I really couldn't blame her if she did. I got on the radio and arranged for a slip at the Destin Yacht Club.

The Destin Yacht Club is the home of Harry T's, a great place to eat. After docking Jaibolero, I did a damage survey. He looked a little ragged around the edges but he wasn't hurt too badly. Some Vetus non-skid was blown loose and the sun-protection material on all the sails was frayed and coming apart. We could re-glue the Vetus and the sails needed restitching anyway. The bimini needed replacing. The leaks around the shroud plates and the mast could be re-sealed with caulking compound. I'm sure Jaibolero lost some bottom paint, but it was too cold to go down and check it out.

Elaine demanded, "We will not leave port until we know there is no foul weather forecast for a week. Your luck is going to run out one of these days." I was always the one who set the goals, who made the major decisions, and who was held responsible for the screwups. She was always along for the ride. As long as everything went along fine, I was in the driver's seat. The way things were at this point, I was about to have my license suspended. It was obvious that she was frustrated with me, and I had to do something to get her in a better mood. A new outfit and good food, that always worked. I told her it was Harry T's for sure tonight. I had promised her Harry T's the night before but, there was no way, we were too exhausted after our ordeal.

We went for a long walk. It was great to get our feet back on the ground. We discussed all the things we had endured the last four days. Almost all of them could have been prevented. I told her, "I am never going to press my luck with the weather again. I have learned my lesson. I will get better charts. I am going to play it so safe from now on that it will get boring." She liked hearing that, but I don't think she believed it.

We went to Yachties that afternoon and I bought her a couple of nice tops on sale. While Elaine went to do laundry, I went to a bar that had a special on raw oysters, a dozen for a dollar and draft beer for a dollar. There were several locals at the bar taking advantage of the special. Bad weather is always good for bar business. They all appeared to be boat people. I squeezed in and placed my order. They were talking about the previous day's storm. One guy said he couldn't believe what he heard on the radio the night before. He said there was some green horn in a sailboat trying to make it over the sandbar during the storm. Another fellow spoke up and said that it must have made it in because there was a sailboat anchored just inside the bay in the middle of the channel early this morning. The first guy said it was impossible. They all agreed that the boat must have sailed on to some other port or gone back out to sea.

In situations like this I should not say anything, but I couldn't help it. I spoke up and said it was my boat, and we made it in. My Kentucky accent caught them by surprise. It was quiet. Nobody said anything. I thought I might be in trouble when this big bearded fellow asked me where I was from. He sounded irritated. I said I was from Kentucky. He reached out and grabbed me by the shoulder and said he was going to buy me a beer. I didn't object. He told the rest of them, "Just leave it up to a Kentucky Hillbilly to come down here and show us how to do things."

I had made some friends. They bought me a couple of more beers. These guys were all right. I found out later that the big one with the beard was from Kentucky, also. I told them how I surfed Jaibolero across the sandbar and they all had a good laugh. The big guy said, "that's one hell of a story." I could tell by the way they were shaking their heads that they didn't believe me. They knew I got him across but they would never believe I surfed him across. No one would probably ever believe me.

When we got back to Jaibolero, the weather forecast was clear skies, 2-foot seas, and 10 to 12-knot winds from the North. With winds from the north we could sail fairly close to shore and it should be like sailing in a pond. Perfect conditions--so I told Elaine we would sail to Pensacola the next morning. She didn't protest so I figured I must still be in the driver's seat.

The sail to Pensacola was perfect. I set the sails and the autopilot and never touched them until we turned into the channel at Pensacola. We read and relaxed all day. Elaine even got a little sun. We docked at a marina and ate a fantastic fish dinner that night at a local restaurant. We saw one of the most beautiful sunsets ever. Thank God for a great day. We were hooked. We had tasted the good life. Some day in the near future we would be cruising.

The next day we motored the intracoastal over to Mobile. It was a nice day with a lot of scenery, but I would rather have been out in the Gulf sailing. Turner Marine in Mobile was to be Jaibolero's home for the next six months. After we had tied up at the dock, some people came over and greeted us. Jaibolero looked pretty ragged with big pieces of Sunbrella material hanging off the two head sails and the bimini ripped in several places. One guy asked if we had been caught out in that bad storm a couple days before. Trying to be macho, I told him that we were in it but, it wasn't so bad, just 70 mph winds, that's all. Elaine shook her head in disgust and told them that it was worse than bad. The eternal optimist that I am, I said it could have been worse. Everyone had a big laugh.

The past week had proved to be a rewarding escapade of trials and triumphs that would remain in our memories forever.

Chapter 6

Our First Overnight Sail

It was Saturday, September 3, 1994. We had owned Jaibolero for almost two years and were finally going cruising. The overnight sail from Panama City to Tampa had been on my mind for months. I was excited beyond imagination. Elaine was apprehensive about sailing at night out of sight of land. In fact, I was having a hard time talking her into going period. I told her, "Several people make this overnight crossing every year. If they can do it, we can do it." Elaine's disapproval was obvious. She stated, "That stupid attitude has kept you in trouble your whole life." After pleading and begging and promising her all kinds of ignorant stuff, I finally talked her into going.

Everything had fallen into place. Jason, our youngest, was settled in as a freshman at the University of Kentucky. I had sold my four businesses and had long-term leases on the properties. We sold our home and bought a smaller one. It was perfect for a retired couple. All the bills were set up on automatic fund transfer. Elaine's sister was to take care of the mail. We had someone to look after the house. Jaibolero, our Offshore 40, looked like new. He had new Vetus non-skid, a new bottom job, new varnish on the teak, the sails refurbished, new canvas and was buffed and waxed. We were ready. Our dream was coming true. Just one thing went wrong, the weather. What should have been a relaxing, therapeutic sail from Panama City to Tampa turned into a demented struggle to survive.

The weather report was favorable. Winds from the west 10-12 knots and 3-5 foot seas. A front from the north was expected by morning but with a mild transition, maximum of 20-knot winds. Jaibolero was full of water, fuel and enough supplies for six months. As we left the pass to Panama City, I knew that for once I was heading into the

Gulf and I was not going to have to turn around and go back after a few hours of sailing. Jaibolero was charging along on a beam reach at 6.5 knots under headsail and main. Some friends, Dan and Janie of Panama City, were anchored out at Shell Island. We stayed in touch with them every 30 minutes to check the range of our VHF's. After about 30 miles we lost communication. They were so envious, they wished they were sailing along with us.

We rounded Cape San Blas around midnight making great time and enjoying the stars. The adrenaline was flowing, neither one of us could think about going to sleep. Our new Navico 8000 autopilot was doing just great. Our new Garmin GPS 45 kept us right on target. We started to get our "sea legs." I noticed some clouds from the NE were covering up the stars. The winds were still from the west so I thought the winds would keep the front from getting to us. Wrong. The clouds just kept on covering up the stars on our port side.

I took the headsail in and put out the staysail. About 1 PM the fireworks started. It was like two gods in the sky, each trying to see which one could throw the most lightning bolts at the other. It was awesome. I thought to myself, I'm glad that stuff is a long ways away. It started at least 20 miles away and we had the best seat in the house. Unfortunately, it kept coming toward us. I wasn't as concerned about the winds as I was the lightning. After our ordeal off Destin in 1992, I was confident Jaibolero could handle strong winds and rough seas. Elaine was expressing some sincere concern. I rolled in about half of the main sail. I told Elaine that, with this set-up we could handle 30 to 35-knot winds and that thunderstorms rarely ever had winds above that. Wrong again. The winds and the seas hit us. There were 40 to 50-knot winds and 15 to 20-foot walls of water slamming into us. I released the main sheet. We were doing max hull speed under staysail alone. I got the main rolled in. There was no way we could hold Jaibolero into or slightly off the wind. We began going through some of the waves. Raw water was hitting the dodger with such force that I thought the new dodger and bimini were going to be ripped off. Elaine had that "deer in the headlights" look again. She had been through this before. I reminded her of the weather forecast. I was not responsible for this storm--it wasn't suppose to happen. I told her it was just another test and that a little prayer couldn't hurt anything. I told her, she had gotten us through worse than this and it was time for her to get busy.

We tried running with the wind for a while, which is normally the best game plan under these conditions. The dingy hung from the davits by chains and I had it tied down with stabilizing lines to keep it from swinging around. The waves were so huge and close together that they began crashing over the dingy. I looked back and the stabilizing lines were ripped off the dingy. The nylon loops on the dingy had failed. It was hanging from the chains and every wave that hit it sent it into some wild gyrations. The davits could not hold up under this abuse. They would be ripped off the back of the boat and could tear gaping holes in the transom. I thought about the sea anchor, but slowing down would have made things worse. We tried a beam reach and Jaibolero was being picked up 15 to 20-feet by each wave and then dropped. This definitely was not good for him. Just as each wave was about to hit us, I would turn the wheel to point him a little into the wind and waves trying to soften the impact. Wave after wave kept breaking over the top of Jaibolero. We put our safety harnesses on to keep us from being washed out of the cockpit. I had heard that bad storms in the Gulf were the worst and now I understand why. In the ocean, 40 to 50-knot winds and 15 to 20-foot seas seem much easier to handle because the waves are so far apart. In the Gulf, the water is so shallow that the waves are much steeper and closer together, which makes it much worse.

After a couple of hours I told Elaine that it couldn't last much longer. Storms like this usually blew right on through. Double wrong. This storm stayed on top of us for 30 "God-for-saken" hours. I like challenges but, this was ridiculous. I could not leave the wheel for one minute. There was no going down below. Elaine and I both started losing our "sea legs." We started taking Dramamine. The beating Jaibolero took was horrible. To hold up under this kind of punishment, he had to be tough. I really didn't know if he would last much longer. I know there is a structural limit to what a boat can take. He had to be approaching that limit. Elaine went below and screamed back up that water was coming in everywhere. I opened the hatchway and looked down below. Raw water was running out through all the electronics at the nav station on the port side and raw water was running down on the counter in the galley and sloshing back and forth on the starboard side. It looked like the leaks were coming from shroud plates, and I hoped it was just the sealant that failed and not structural damage.

I was at the wheel for 24 hours, soaked to the bone, cold and tired beyond description. Finally, the winds slacked off a little. They were still about 30 knots and the seas were bad. We were heading in the general vicinity of Tampa. For the first time since the storm hit, I felt I could trust the autopilot. It was now late Sunday night and I laid down in the floor of the cockpit to try and get some rest. We had our safety harnesses on and the autopilot was doing a pretty good job considering the conditions. I asked Elaine to stay awake and make sure we did not run into anything. We didn't have radar. I went to sleep thinking Elaine was on watch. Wrong again. She had laid down on the floor beside me and gone to sleep. The next thing I know we both woke up with fish flopping around in the cockpit. Getting fish in the cockpit of a high topsides, center cockpit boat was a real feat. The waves were still so big that when Jaibolero was in a trough between waves, flying fish were flying into the cockpit. My heart skipped more than a few beats. We looked at each other and both thought the same thing; people aren't going to believe this. Once we pitched the fish out of the cockpit and back in the water, we both had a good laugh.

About 8 AM Monday morning the winds were back to 15 to 25-knots, but the seas were still very mixed up. By noon the winds had died, and we motored for the next three hours. We dropped hook at John's Pass just north of Tampa. It was time to enjoy a respite from the "sail from hell." We were beat up and exhausted. Elaine cooked us dinner. She was very quiet. Finally she said, "We are staying right here for several days. Some one up there is trying to tell us we are not suppose to be sailors." I told her, "I was never worried because I knew her prayers would pull us through. Most people never see a miracle and we've seen several since we started sailing." If looks could kill, I would be dead. Elaine was showing strong symptoms of "port sickness" again. Deep down I knew this should be the end to our cruising! No woman in her right mind would continue on after the "hang-on-for-your-life" ordeals I had put her through.

We stayed at John's Pass for a couple of days and worked on some projects that happened as a result of the storm. We had developed leaks around the shroud plates and at the mast. Salt water got in the single side band radio and knocked it out of commission. I flushed the rest of the electronics off with fresh water and hoped they would be okay. Elaine expressed a concern for not being able to get the weather reports. I told her, "We can probably get all the weather info we need from the VHF. Besides that, after what we have just been through, no one in their right mind would believe the weather men again anyway. You've got to believe that everything turns out for the best, that there is a reason for everything. We have been tested. We have survived two major storms at sea, and my confidence in my boat and our abilities has maxed out." Elaine said, "That's what really worries me."

I finally convinced Elaine that we couldn't stay at John's Pass forever. We continued on down to Venice. Thank goodness we were hit with a 35 to 40-knot thunderstorm just outside the entrance to Venice so I could demonstrate my expert seamanship by "hoving-to" for about an hour until the storm passed. It was neat. I backed the staysail out and turned the wheel all the way to port and we just floated along with our hatches battened down just as snug as a bug in a rug. When the winds died down we were about a half a mile from the entrance to Venice. We had great stops at Venice, Ft. Myers, Naples and Marco Island before our next overnight sail to Key West. Elaine was starting to really enjoy the cruising life.

We left Marco Island headed for Key West at 4:30 in the afternoon and motorsailed. At 8:30 that night the winds picked up to 10 to 12-knots from the SE. We cut the engine off and sailed close-hauled at 6+ knots all night. The seas were almost calm. The moon and stars were beyond description. I sat on the windward side, with my legs hanging over the side, and let the autopilot do the work. This is what makes it all worth while. When it came time to get Elaine up for her watch, I let her sleep. I was selfish. I wanted this night all to myself. We arrived in Key West about 7:30 AM and dropped the hook about 9 AM. It was a wonderful night, one I would never forget; our first overnight sail that didn't end up in a struggle to survive.

Key West was one of our favorite stops. The architecture was great. We loved walking the old streets and checking out the restorations. And then there was "Sloppy Joe's" -- always a fun place to visit. Our favorite place was Mallory Dock where everyone goes to watch the sunset hopeing to see the green flash. Every afternoon there were numerous performers (tightrope acts, escape artists, musicians, etc.) starting about 5 PM.

Our next stop in the Keys was Marathon. We only stayed there a couple nights before going on to Key Largo.

It was September 23 and we were sailing from Key Largo to Miami. I could see the skyscrapers of Miami off my port bow and another one of those storms was brewing on my starboard side. After a few days in Miami we planned to jump over and cruise the Bahamas for a few months.

Chapter 7

Our first night in the Bahamas

We left Panama City on September 3 and arrived in Miami on September 23. Storms and rain for twenty days. Well, it did not stop when we reached Miami. It stormed and rained for ten more days. So much for the sunshine state. This rain seemed to go on forever. All the locals said they had never seen it rain for so long, that this was a record. We had been cruising for 30 days and it had been storming on us for 30 days. My optimism was fading. Everyday Elaine pointed up at the wet heavens and said, "Someone up there keeps sending you a message and you won't listen." I was beginning to believe her when on the thirtieth day they forecasted sunshine and southwest winds. We got ready to make our first Gulf Stream crossing just in case the weather forecasters got lucky. I set the alarm for 5 AM and awoke to a sky full of stars. God must have heard mine and thousands of other's prayers.

We pulled anchor and motored out of Biscayne Bay. We left the Miami Channel at 7 AM with 20-plus-knot winds from the SW. Crossing the Gulfstream can really be tough if the wind direction, weather conditions and sea conditions are not just right. The prevailing winds are from the southeast and the current between Florida and the Bahamas is 2 to 3-knots from south to north. Bimini is only about 50 miles due east of Miami. If you have a sailboat that can motor at 5-knots and head due east, you would miss Bimini by 25 to 30-miles to the north. When figuring the heading this has to be taken into account. The other thing is that you end up motoring into the waves trying to offset the effect of the current. This slows you down even more and makes the current have even a bigger effect. For this reason most sailboats leave Miami about 10 PM and arrive in Bimini some time the next afternoon.

Southwest winds were forecast and we were on a beam reach. It seemed to this hillbilly sailor to be the perfect time for crossing the Gulfstream. There were a lot of boats waiting to make the crossing. I kept looking back for other sails wondering why nobody else was making the crossing. I found out later.

We flew across the Gulfstream in less than seven hours. I bragged to Elaine how great her captain and her boat was. These southwest winds were great for getting across the Gulfstream. What I didn't realize was that they also made it impossible to get into Bimini harbor. I've got to learn to read the cruising guides and do as these people say. The cruising guide says not to attempt the channel into Bimini in strong offshore winds, strong westerly winds in this case. What is meant by strong? Are strong winds over 10 knots, over 20 knots, over 30 knots or what? I learned the hard way what is meant by strong. I now know that 10 to 12-knots is strong and anything over that is too strong. We got one hell of a scare when we started hitting bottom trying to make it through the channel into the harbor at Bimini. How embarrassing it would have been to beach my boat on the first day in the Bahamas. I could just see it being beaten to shreds by the waves. There was no way I was ever going to be able to face my friends and family again. What made things worse was the fact that I had no insurance. Because of the losses from Hurricane Andrew, all the insurance companies had tightened up and none of them thought this hillbilly had enough experience. I had put us in one hell of a predicament.

I knew getting into Bimini was not going to be a piece of cake but hundreds of other boats do it every year so I figured we could make it. The channel had six feet depth at low water. There is a sand bar that extends south from North Bimini for about a mile parallel to South Bimini and the channel is very narrow and right next to South Bimini beach. I could see waves breaking over the sand bar. I lined up the markers and turned exactly where the cruising guide said. There was no way of telling how big the waves were in the channel until we were right on top of them and by then I had already committed myself. I could not believe this channel was so close to the beach. About half way in the channel Jaibolero started bouncing off the bottom. A boat drawing 5 feet 3 inches should go through a channel that has a minimum of 6 feet depth in calm water. However, the waves in the channel were at least 2 feet which puts the depth under 5 feet at times. I didn't have to be a rocket scientist to figure out that Jaibolero was in big trouble if I didn't do something quickly. I pushed the throttle wide open, red-lined the engine, and spun the wheel. I knew from past experience that, as long as I kept him moving, we had a better chance of surviving. I spun him around in the narrow channel. We were so close to the beach I could have jumped to shore and not gotten my feet wet. Jaibolero hit bottom again and almost stopped. The next wave lifted him up and we started moving again. This cycle of dragging bottom and breaking free continued for what seemed like an eternity. If we ever stopped completely, we would end up on the beach for sure. This was definitely another religious experience for me. If I wasn't praying now, I wasn't ever going to pray. Elaine was awfully quiet. She was in deep thought. She was either praying or she was planning on killing me. Luckily, we made it back out to deep water and decided to find an anchorage elsewhere. Somebody must be watching over us.

Our only choice was to motor 10 miles south to Gun Cay. Another one of those things that sounds simple but, it wasn't. We had to motor into 8 to 10 feet seas, 25-knot winds and a strong current, to try to make it to Gun Cay Cut. Even with the engine near red-line, the GPS showed we were making about one knot net over the ground most of the time. After taking a severe beating for a few hours, we finally made the Cat Cay/Gun Cay Cut. We made it around behind Gun Cay and anchored just as the sun was setting. If we had been 30 minutes later, it would have been dark and there is no way I would have attempted this cut in the dark. I guess we would have sailed back to Miami and that would have been the end to our cruising. I cannot explain in words how good it felt to know we were safe at anchor and all Jaibolero had was a little more paint scraped off his keel. It was time to celebrate. Elaine cooked a great supper (Ragu spaghetti). This day had its moments but, in a way, it was very rewarding. I couldn't help but brag a little to Elaine. I told her, "Life is a learning experience and we learned a lot today. A smart person learns from his mistakes and I am getting smarter every day." She told me, "If it takes mistakes and risking our lives to make you smarter, then I wish you would stay dumb." I thought to myself, how could she have said that to me after I had saved her life again?

Chapter 8

The Explorers

We went through customs the next day at Cat Cay. The weather eased up enough so we could get back to Bimini. With the winds at about 15 knots from the north, the channel into Bimini was passable. Our friends, David and Pat from Miami, were planning on running their fishing boat over if the seas settled down. We were really looking forward to doing some serious fishing. We needed to learn how to fish. If it wasn't for the thought of having fresh fish everyday, Elaine probably would have never agreed to cruising. Pat was going to show us how to catch fish and how to clean them. The weather forecasted northern winds for several days and that was the end of our fishing lessons. Elaine was disappointed. I told her, "I will get a book on fishing. After all, that's how I learned to sail." She laughed and said we would starve. I told her she was a world champion at low blows.

We stayed on the hook at Bimini for a few more days. We could not believe how clear the water was. We could see all kinds of fish, barracuda and sea rays swimming under our boat. We dingied to shore and went for some nice walks. Their season had not started yet so there wasn't a lot going on. We didn't care, we just loved being in the Bahamas. We met a neat couple from Key West, Gary and Terri, and their son Bobby. Chronologically, Bobby was only six, but mentally we were on about the same level, in our early teens. We became buddies. Gary was a professional tarpon fisherman and they lived anchored out on their sailboat. These were real experienced boat people. Bobby was even born on their boat. I mean delivered on the boat. Each year, during Gary's off season, they cruised the Bahamas. What a life, either fishing or cruising.

After they heard some of our war stories, they asked us to go across the banks over to Nassau with them. It was obvious they thought we could learn a little something from them. We motored back over to Cat Cay and dropped anchor long enough to have dinner. About 7:30 PM we pulled anchor and motored. There was no wind. The water was slick as glass. There were a zillion stars out but no moon. It was dark and kind of spooky at first. The water glowed on each side of the boat. The phosphorescence was breath taking. It looked like there were a million lightening bugs swimming in the water.

Motoring across the banks that night was a great experience. I started realizing how it felt to be released from all the pressures of the businesses and everything else that kept me in a "wad" all the time. I had just finished reading a book in two days. At home I couldn't even get close to finishing a book. I would catch myself turning pages and not knowing what was on the pages I had just read. My mind was always jumping from one problem to the next. I did not know what it was like to be happy and content. I had too many irons in the fire and couldn't turn things over to my employees--I had to be the one to make all the decisions. I had three businesses at one time and tried to run them all by myself. Elaine said I never listened to anyone. I only heard what I wanted to hear. Everything else floated right by. I told myself this night under the stars was the night my new life would start. No more hustling and worrying for me. This workaholic was now a relaxaholic. I was going to become a good listener. Peace and contentment lookout, I was on the way!

We dropped hook at Chub Cay about 10 the next morning. We went snorkeling on the reef off Mamma Rhoda Rock and it was great. The water was warm and crystal clear. The colors of the different fishes and the coral was spectacular. Some of the fish were even smiling. It was like pictures I had seen in National Geographic. The coral was just a couple feet below the surface in several areas. I saw two sailboat keels on the bottom. That's what happens when you screw up over here. The coral was not very forgiving.

The gentleman on the boat anchored behind us speared a 15-pound grouper with his Hawaiian sling. I had to get me one of those things. Supper was swimming all around us. Gary picked up a few conch and Terri fixed us some conch fritters from her special recipe. They were great. This was the life.

The next day we sailed over to Nassau. We stayed in a marina next to the fish and vegetable markets. Some hard-looking characters hang out around those places. We did not feel very safe that night even though the marina had a guard. The guard looked about sixteen years old. We were glad to get out of there. We didn't like marinas. It was much nicer to be anchored out.

Gary, Terri, and Bobby sailed toward the Exumas. We headed to Eleuthera. We told them that we would see them in Georgetown in about three weeks. It was a perfect day for sailing. Winds from the southeast at 15 knots put us on a beam reach all the way there. We passed by the sunken freighter on the reef at Little Egg Island and headed for Royal Island off North Eleuthera. We were headed for Spanish Wells, but Royal Island sounded so good in the cruising guide we decided to drop anchor there. I don't know how an anchorage could be any better. It was big, deep, easy to enter and protected from winds from any direction.

Royal Island was a very interesting place if you like ruins and exploring. About 60 years ago a wealthy railroad man named Stewart built a mansion with guest houses, care-taker residences, storage buildings, maintenance shops and miles of rock and concrete walking trails. He even built a billiard parlor separate from the house. It has all been deteriorating since his death. You would have thought Elaine and I had discovered an ancient, unexplored ruins on some Mediterranean Island. We were excited and exploring like two kids.

We decided to try and find the beach on the north side of the island. We found a concrete and rock path that we thought would lead us to the beach. The plants and trees almost made the path impassable. There were huge spiders and spider webs every few feet along the path. It was frightening. I had goose bumps all over me. We walked for a considerable distance through what looked like a jungle. Elaine started complaining about being afraid. Brave me told her there wasn't a thing to be a afraid of and that there wasn't anything on this island that would hurt us. No sooner were the words out of my mouth when something very close to us started running through the woods and underbrush. I thought my heart was going to jump out of my chest. I knew it was no cat or chicken. It was a lot bigger and I couldn't tell if it was running toward us or away from us. I sure wasn't going to hang around and find out. Elaine had already split and I was right behind her. She sure can move when she wants to.

It was a good half mile back to the dingy and she never slowed up. When she reached the concrete pier she stopped and gave me a look that could kill. I could tell that she had wet all over herself. I was laughing so hard I couldn't say a thing. She accused me of trying to get her killed. It was obvious that I was not going to hear the end of this. I tried to tell her it was a cat or chicken and I couldn't believe she was afraid. The more I laughed the madder she got. We found out later there were some wild goats on the island. I still think it could have been a mountain lion or a bear. Whew!

This incident reminded me of something funny that had happened to us a few weeks earlier at John's Pass, just north of Tampa. We stayed there a couple of days after our sail over from Panama City. We had dingied in to eat at a restaurant on the south side of the channel. Across the water on the other side are several neat shops. Elaine wanted to go shopping after dinner. We could either dingy across or walk across the draw bridge. Elaine was not going to walk across the draw bridge. She is terrified of heights, and walking on that metal grate that raised up to let the boats through, was completely out of the question. I was determined to show her that she was being ridiculous and there was nothing to be afraid of. I told her that if we get in the dingy, we were going back to the boat. I said I didn't want to go shopping anyway, I hate shopping. That did it. She was going to see that I suffered. She said she would cross that *?#@^&* draw bridge.

As we were passing the bridge attendant's little building, I told her to run like crazy if the horn blows because that draw bridge will come up quickly. I think the attendant heard me because, when we got exactly in the middle of the draw bridge, the horn went off. I was about half way expecting it and it still scared me. Elaine threw her arms up in the air, screamed, and took off running like greased lightening. She was across the bridge in half a second. I was laughing so hard I couldn't run. When I got to the other side Elaine was waiting for me. I couldn't help it, I could not stop laughing. It was the funniest thing I had ever seen. I said come on, let's go shopping. She just stood there and said she couldn't. She had these big tears in her eyes and she was standing kind of straddle legged. I looked down and she was soaked. She had wet all over herself. She blamed it all on me, as usual.

It was a beautiful and peaceful night anchored out at Royal Island. I laughed out loud several times that night thinking about our episode in the woods. Elaine had nightmares all night long about monsters chasing her through the woods. I went to sleep thinking about seeing Spanish Wells the next day and snorkeling the Devil's Backbone Reef. I slept like a rock. There was a nice little breeze, but the boat never moved. It was like we were on a duck pond all night.

Chapter 9

Exploring Eleuthera

We motored the eight miles over to Spanish Wells and dropped anchor on the east end next to Charles Island. Every anchorage there had a major problem. There was no speed limit in the harbor or channel. These crazy people ran their boats wide open through the harbor all hours of the day and night. They haul workers over to Eleuthera starting about five in the morning. The faster their boat was, the more runs they could make; the more people they could haul, the more money they made. This went on until late at night. They must have been in a bad mood because they have to get up early, so they took it out on the people anchored in the harbor. They would run by Jaibolero doing at least 40 mph and not missing us by five feet. They would go out of their way just to buzz a boat anchored out. We were looking forward to leaving this place.

It was an eleven-mile trip to get to Dunmore Town on Harbour Island. It had to be the toughest 11 miles to navigate in the Bahamas. There were numerous coral heads and reefs all the way across the north end of Eleuthera. There were few markers and they couldn't be trusted. The Cruising Guide said to use a local pilot and then only under favorable weather conditions. We played it safe and decided to dingy over. We left about nine in the morning. It was a long, rough 60-minute dingy ride. After seeing the reefs and coral heads, I would think a stranger would have a slim chance of making the trip in a sail-boat without major damage or sinking.

Dunmore Town was one of the major winter resorts in the Bahamas. We loved it. The architecture and the plant life was fabulous. On the Atlantic side were numerous homes overlooking their famous pink beach. It lived up to its reputation. It was the prettiest beach we had ever seen. The sand was so soft and fluffy we sank down to our ankles. We both agreed that, if we ever stopped sailing, we could live here. We only had this one day here so we tried to see it all. We walked and walked. We left about 3 PM for the long dingy ride back. The winds had picked up in the afternoon, as usual, which made for a terribly bumpy and wet ride back.

When we got back to Spanish Wells, I pulled the dingy up to the city dock and found a fishing boat that had just come in. We bought five pounds of fresh "hog" snapper. We cooked it on the grill. It was fantastic. We had enough left over for two more meals.

The next day we went out and snorkeled the Devil's Backbone Reef. I didn't know there were so many different fish. There were sea turtles and one took me for a ride. There was a five-foot barracuda following us around for a while. I have read that they won't harm humans but this one looked and acted hungry. We tried to ignore him. He continued to follow us. Finally, I swam toward him as fast as I could under water. He did what he was supposed to do and took off. Elaine snorkeled for about an hour and I snorkeled for about another hour while she sat in the dingy and warmed in the sun. This was one of the most enjoyable things either of us had ever experienced.

The speed boats woke us up early the next morning. I had seen enough of these lunatics. We pulled anchor at first daylight and headed down to Current Cut for the Bight of Eleuthera. We sailed across to Hatchet Bay and anchored for the night. Not much there but a few destroyed sailboats half sunk on the banks thanks to Hurricane Andrew. We sailed down to Governor's Harbour and dropped the hook. We were the only sailboat anchored there. This was the wrong time of the year. We walked for hours checking out the neat old homes, Club Med and the beautiful beach. Elaine ended up with shin splints.

When we got back to the wharf some fishermen were laying out their daily catch. As Elaine and I were inspecting their catch, I commented that those sure were some big lobster. He looked up at me and said, "These are crawfish, mon." I told him they sure don't grow that big in Kentucky. The crawfish in our creeks don't get over three inches long. He continued laying out his catch and just shook his head. I found out a few days later that their crawfish were really lobster.

The Cruising Guide stated that there was poor holding in Governor's Harbour. They were not joking. The winds swung around from the west. We had two anchors out in 20-knot winds and were dragging. We moved up behind Levi Island for protection. The holding wasn't much better there so we sailed on down to Rock Sound.

The weather kept us at Rock Sound for three days. We were the only cruisers anchored there. By the third day Elaine was about to drive me nuts. She wanted to see parts of the island that we couldn't get to by boat. She wanted to see the very exclusive Cotton Bay area and Windemere Island where Princess Diana stayed. Friendly Bob let us rent his best car. Really, it didn't drive too badly for a '79 Le Mans with 280,000 miles. The problem was that these people drive on the wrong side of the road. For thirty-five years I've been driving on the right side of the road, which was right, and now I'm supposed to drive on the wrong side, which was the left side, and the wrong side is the right side. This Kentucky Hillbilly had a hard time with this. Most of the roads were so narrow that everybody drove in the middle until they met another vehicle. The only way I could make myself stay on the wrong side was to continually say over and over, "You stay on my side of the road and I'll stay on yours." I was doing pretty good until the first time I came to an intersection and was going to turn. It was difficult to turn a corner and stay on the wrong side. My instincts kept telling me I was wrong.

Now I understand why all their vehicles look like they are several-time losers of a demolition derby. When two vehicles meet on a narrow road somebody was supposed to yield. We never saw the first car yield. They just kept driving head on until the last possible second and then they both ran two wheels in the ditch and missed each other by inches. They whipped back up on the road and just kept on driving and smiling like nothing ever happened. They must have been playing a mental game. If they stopped smiling or slowed down, they would lose.

The main highway on Eleuthera was the Queen's Highway and it was a little wider. There was no speed limit here or, if there was, there was no one to enforce it and the honor system wasn't working. I was driving a safe speed and vehicles were going by us so fast that I felt like I was driving a golf cart in the Indy 500. There weren't any "no passing" lines painted on the hills and curves. The government knew it would be a waste of money. These people passed on top of hills and in blind curves. They have no fear. They drove like they have nothing to live for. I ran off the road more than once that day trying to save our lives. I admit that I get us in most of our dangerous predicaments but I can blame this one on Elaine. We were both very glad to get back on Jaibolero.

The next day we sailed over to Cape Eleuthera at Powell Point. This required some alert navigating. This trip required seven heading changes which had to be at the right place or we were in big trouble. Maneuvering through the coral heads was like trying to get through a mine field. Elaine was on the bow as lookout the whole trip. Our luck held out. It had been several days since we had been in one of our special kind of predicaments on the boat. I couldn't help but brag a little. Elaine was afriad I would jinx us again.

Chapter 10

Ben and Kenny

Cape Eleuthera Marina was part of the resort that previously included restaurants, rental cottages, condominiums, golf course and exclusive building lots. The place folded a few years back but the marina was still being operated. It doesn't have a phone or groceries or much else. There's one thing this place had and that's world champion mosquitoes. When the sun goes down, you better be in your boat with the screens up. These mosquitoes really go for hillbilly blood. The first night there I decided I would go out for a little walk. I didn't make it fifty feet before I was completely covered by these blood-sucking little varmints. They were well trained. They swarm you and then their leader gives the signal to all bite at once. Elaine was real pleased with me when I jumped down below and closed the hatch. I must have brought at least a hundred down below with me. We were chasing mosquitoes all night.

Elaine's mother and stepfather were both sick and we needed to get to a phone to check on them. The next night Kenny, the female dockmaster, was taking a couple into town for supplies and offered to give Elaine and I a ride. Since the nearest phone was 20 miles away, we accepted the offer. It was really nice of her but one look at her car and I balked. I know when a car is a death trap and we were getting into one. I told Elaine we should pass but she insisted and we got in the back seat. The only thing worse than driving on this island was riding with a Bahamian at night, for about 20 miles, on a road that hasn't had any repair for 20 years, in a car that was beyond repair 20 years ago. Honestly, Kenny's car had four warning lights on the dash and three of them glowed all the time. The other one glowed when she put on the brakes. There were no door panels on the back doors and the window cranks were missing. If you wanted the back windows up, you reached in the door and pulled them up and held them. The back seat springs were totally shot, it was as if we were sitting on the floorboard. I knew one thing for sure, this was going to be a long ride, or a short ride and a long walk.

Bahamians think nothing about stopping in the middle of the road and talking, day or night. We came around a corner doing what seemed like 150 miles per hour and there were four head lights stopped directly in front of us. It didn't take long to figure out that these four head lights didn't belong to the same vehicle. It was two cars stopped side by side on a very narrow road. I saw the red brake light flash on the dash a couple of times as Kenny pumped the brakes. We didn't slow down much. We found out later that her brakes had not worked right for a couple of years. I don't know what happened next because I ducked down behind the front seat. The car turned left real quick and we jumped a ditch and shot up a bank. I heard gravel and bushes hitting the car and we bounced around quite a bit. Kenny never quit laughing. We jumped back on the road and never slowed down. This was insanity. I could see the headlines in the paper back home, "Cruising couple from Kentucky dies in the Bahamas while hitching a ride to call and see if their relatives were feeling better."

We made it to the store. The other couple went shopping and Elaine and I went down the street a few blocks to use the only pay phone in town. When we got back to the store, the other couple was paying for their supplies, $280 worth. I told them there was no way to get all of that in the trunk of that little car. I was right. I rode back with a case of motor oil and a case of cokes in my lap and three boxes of groceries stacked to the roof between Elaine and I. We stopped at Friendly Bob's tavern. Then I had a case of oil, a case of cokes, and two cases of beer in my lap. That was okay because now I couldn't see where we were going. I thought I was permanently paralyzed by the time we got back to the marina. Jaibolero never looked so good.

Before we left on this shakedown cruise, I had visions of eating fresh fish everyday that we would catch ourselves. It had been six weeks since we'd left Panama City and the only fish we'd eaten was what we'd bought. Elaine reminded me daily that, if we depended on my fishing for food, we would starve. Well, things changed at Cape Eleuthera. We met "Ben the Fisherman." Ben took Elaine and I fishing, conching and lobstering. We put all the gear, the rod and reels, the hand lines, the snorkeling equipment, etc., in the dingy and headed out to catch supper. We trolled on the way out to the reefs. We used some little, clear, fake shrimp and Elaine caught three nice yellow tails in just a few minutes. I had used these little fake shrimp before and never caught anything. Ben made it look easy. It was unbelievable. It was one of the best days of our lives. We went to some reefs and Ben showed me how to find and spear lobster with a Hawaiian sling. This guy could free dive down 20 feet looking under the ledges for lobster and stay for at least two minutes. I was barely able to go down that far and then I had to go right back up. Ben said I needed some bigger fins like his. I replied, "Bigger fins and bigger lungs."

Ben asked Elaine how many lobsters she wanted and she said six. Six big ones was what we got. It was amazing, he brought one up on almost every dive. We went further out and dove for some conch. He showed us how to clean them and what parts to use for bait. The locals eat the conch raw. Raw conch may be the ugliest, nastiest looking thing on planet earth. I love raw oysters and I am usually game for anything, once. I tried to be macho and take a little bite but every time I got it near my mouth I would just about upchuck my breakfast. There was no way Ben was going to except this, so I finally gave in and took a bite and swallowed as fast as I could. It was tough to keep it down but somehow I managed.

We dropped anchor behind some coral heads next to a small island. Ben had chopped up a bunch of conch and he chummed the area. I'd never heard of this. Chumming is taking a bunch of fish food and throwing it out in an area to attract the fish. I've never seen anything like it. The fish were churning up the water like an agitator washer. No sooner than the bait hit the water we had a fish on the line. We caught yellow tail, grouper, trigger fish and a barracuda. Ben wanted the cuda for strip bait. When the dingy got full, we quit. Next came the cleaning lesson back on Ben's fishing boat. I flunked. Ben told me, "no worry mon, no worry, you be o-kay." We'll never forget Ben.

Ben and Elaine before cleaning lesson.

Chapter 11

Exumas and Georgetown

We left Cape Eleuthera and sailed over to Highborne Cay in the Exumas. The snorkeling at Highborne Cay was about as good as it gets. We stopped at Staniel Cay and at Farmer's Cay on the way down to Georgetown. We really enjoyed the Exumas, they were everything we expected and more. The Exuma Cays consist of about 360 cays that stretch over 90 miles. Great Exuma Island adds about another 40 miles. Most of the cays were small and primitive with very few settlements. The Exumas have some of the most beautiful anchoring spots and some of the nicest beaches in the world. We have seen several ruins of what were once great plantations. Iguanas ate out of our hands. Barracudas have chased us while we were snorkeling. The waters were the clearest in the world and the colors of the coral reefs were fabulous. The Exumas lived up to their reputation. Georgetown, the main settlement in the Exumas, was our final destination on our shakedown cruise before we headed back to the States. When we arrived, there were about 40 boats on the hook and a few more at the marina. During the peak season, Georgetown hosts over 400 cruising boats. Even in the off season, something was going on all the time; potlucks, volleyball, etc. At least three of the bars have a satellite dish, and everyone goes and watches the games on Sunday afternoon.

We met some real nice people, people that we will remember forever. We will never see most of them again. We all know that it's just a temporary friendship, but it's special because of the circumstances. Everyone learns from everybody else. Everyone listens to channel 16 on their VHF. If anyone needs information, they just ask. Everybody also knows what everybody else is doing. When someone calls someone else on 16, they then switch to another channel to talk. Everybody else switches too. There are no secrets in the sailing community. There was a Halloween party at Two Turtles and I got on the radio to find out when these friends were going. We switched to another channel. She told me what their outfits were and asked what we were going to wear? I thought for a minute and said we didn't really have any outfits and I guess we would go as nudists. That night everybody had some comment about our conversation. I now know that they all listen and its not just Elaine listening in on everybody else.

A couple from New York and Elaine and I arranged for a tour of the island of Great Exuma. Will Nixon (no kin to Richard) was the guide. Mr. Nixon was a "live wire" for a 74 year old. He was 100% Bahamian and a descendant of slaves. He showed us the slave quarters where his grandparents lived while slaves on a large plantation. He has 14 kids by his first wife who is deceased. He can't keep up with how many great grand children he has but it's a lot. He has remarried and we met his second wife. I accused him of robbing the cradle because she was only forty. He said he used the "stick logic" for getting a new wife. I told him I didn't think I had heard of that before. He told me, if he had married an old woman his age and he dropped his stick, then who would pick it up? He had to have a younger woman to pick up his stick when he dropped it. He also said that two dead batteries can't start an engine. I thought to myself, this guy makes a lot of sense. By the way, he started a new family with his second wife. They have a three year old. Elaine asked him how many more kids he wanted? He said he thought he was through, he said, "I've parked my car." Can you imagine having your kids and your great grand kids in the same class in school?

Mr. Nixon also helped me to understand part of what was wrong with the Bahamian economy. I am always on the lookout for an opportunity, but this place was scary. Nothing seems to survive here. Failed housing developments, restaurants and motels are everywhere. The government here will allow outside investors but they must hire Bahamians from the management down. You must use local architects and contractors. It's not unusual for it to take three years to finish a house. Half the houses here never do get finished. It took so long to finish larger projects, they were dilapidated and run down before they even opened. They take this "no hurry, no worry, mon" thing seriously. Mr. Nixon said that everybody wants a paper and a pen and nobody knows how to grow anything anymore. I asked him what that meant? Will said they all want to be managers and no one wants to work. He said, "Anyone can say they are a manager but that don't make it so." I liked this guy.

Typical of the Bahamian's attitude is the sign advertising the hours at the Ocean Cabin Restaurant on Little Farmer's Cay: "We open most days about 9 or 10, occasionally as early as 7; but some days as late as 12 or 1. We close about 5 or 6 or maybe about 4 or 5. Some days or afternoons we aren't here at all and lately we've been here about all the time except when we are some place else but we might be here then, too."

We headed back to the States for the holidays. We left Jaibolero at Key Largo from Thanksgiving until after the first of the year. We thought about sailing down to the Virgin Islands, Caribbean, Venezuela, Central America and Mexico. Or maybe just sail back over to Georgetown and hang out for a while. Or maybe just stop just about anywhere and drop anchor and just stay awhile. Or we might just sail to just about any of those places I mentioned earlier and stay awhile or we could just stay a pretty long time which might be a few weeks or several months. I think I've caught the Bahamian attitude.

Chapter 12

Hurricane Gordon

While on the way back across the Bahama Banks we heard some discouraging weather reports from other boats that could pick up the Nassau weather station. There was a tropical wave coming that could possibly upgrade to a tropical storm. Once it becomes a tropical storm there was always a chance it would be upgraded even further and become a hurricane. Our single side band radio has not worked since salt water got into it during the storm the first night we left Panama City and the VHF only had a range of about 5 miles due to a bad connection at the antenna which we discovered later. Elaine kept expressing her concern about our radios. My come back was that Christopher Columbus never had any radios and look what he did. I told Elaine that with our luck this thing will turn into a hurricane and the only thing that God hadn't tested us with so far was a full fledged hurricane. Elaine said I would find one and sail us right into the middle of it just to have something to write about. I asked her if she ever got bored. She ignored me. I told her my biggest fear in life was that she would get bored and leave me for somebody exciting. She continued to ignore me. I think I finally got the best of her.

Elaine has depended on me for years to get her safely from one place to another. I hadn't really thought about being responsible for her safety when we were traveling in a motorized vehicle down the highway. She thought I was a good driver and she trusted me. We just got in the vehicle and went. It was an assumption that I didn't dwell on. It's different on a sailboat. She felt she was putting her life on the line. Elaine's well-being depended on my good judgement, and she wouldn't let me forget it. She kept telling me all her friends thought she was truly brave to get on a sailboat and take off cruising.

It was hard for me to understand this at first but, after a couple of months cruising, I was beginning to see where she was coming from.

About 5:30 in the morning on November 11, we pulled anchor at Chub Cay and sailed across the banks toward Gun Cay. We should have made Gun Cay just before dark. Our plans were to anchor one night at Gun Cay and then sail to Key Largo. When we arrived at Gun Cay about 7:30 that night, we decided to make the cut between Gun Cay and Cat Cay and sail to Key Largo without stopping. Two things helped us make that decision. The first was the weather; the wind direction was perfect for an overnight sail to Key Largo. The second was a boat in the Gun Cay anchorage said that the weather station in Nassau had reported the tropical wave would hit Nassau in two days. It was still a tropical wave and had not been upgraded, yet. Nassau reported a slim chance for an upgrade. Nassau did not know my luck. With no real safe anchorages (hurricane holes) in the Cat Cay, Gun Cay or Bimini area, it only made sense to keep going. This decision rates right up there as one of the best I've ever made.

There was a 10 to 12-knot breeze from the southeast all night and all we had to do was keep an eye open for other boats. It was a beautiful sail that night, lots of stars. The next morning the winds almost died on us. We were battling a two-knot current in the Gulfstream. At times we were lucky to be doing four knots which left us doing only about two knots over the ground. If the wind had kept blowing at least 10 knots, we would have easily been at anchor in Key Largo before dark. Now, we were faced with zig-zagging our way across the coral in the dark to get to Key Largo. This was what I thought was going to be our main problem. Wrong.

Late that afternoon I turned on the radio and could get the weather station. That tropical wave was now Hurricane Gordon and he was heading our way in a big hurry. It started getting dark and we were still a few miles from Key Largo. The shallow area between the Florida Keys and the Atlantic Ocean is Hawk's Channel. You have to be real careful here because the Atlantic Ocean just off Hawk's Channel is a major shipping lane for ships from the Pacific Ocean coming through the Panama Canal and heading to the east coast of the U.S. or to Europe. This area always has lots of freighters and tankers. The closer we came to Hawk's Channel, the more lights we saw, and these lights were moving. It was unbelievable. There was a traffic jam in the north-bound shipping lane. There were freighters, huge tankers, cruise ships, luxury yachts, fishing boats and other boats all bow to stern going lickety-split for as far as we could see in both directions. They were trying to get into port before Hurricane Gordon hit. Elaine asked me how we were going to get to Key Largo and get anchored. I really didn't know.

I turned to channel 16 on the VHF and there were a thousand people all trying to talk at once. Channel 16 is used by marine traffic for hailing and emergencies. It didn't help matters that we were just about out of fuel. We idled along for a couple of hours waiting for an opening to cross between two ships. It takes miles for one of these big ships to slow down. You can't just pull out in front of one of these suckers and expect them to slam on the brakes. The big tankers and freighters had a little more distance between each other but it was still going to be risky. Out in open water I try to stay as far away from big ships as I can. It was obvious we had to get dangerously close just to get between them. The closer we got to them the more confident I was that we could make it across safely. Convincing Elaine was something else. It all boiled down to timing. Our best bet was to go along close beside one of the big ships in the opposite direction they are heading and, as soon as that one passed, I would push the throttle wide open and turn in front of the next one. Most frightening things that happen to a person happen so quickly that you don't really have time to get scared until it's over. This was different. I don't know how long it took, it probably wasn't long, but it seemed like it took about an hour for us to get across, in front of and clear of that gigantic tanker. What a way to finish the final leg of our shakedown cruise.

We dropped anchor at about 11 PM off Key Largo. The marina at Key Largo has a few slips along the wall and a few more "stern to" slips for small boats. The marina was on a canal and there was one small place at the far end for turn arounds. There would be no way anyone could turn a sailboat around in that small place in strong winds. This meant trouble if no slips were available along the wall. There was no way of knowing if a slip was available without going in and we couldn't risk that. We had no other choice except to stay on anchor out in the bay. The winds started picking up shortly after midnight. The holding at Key Largo was terrible. The anchors started dragging. I worked all night long at trying to get the anchors to hold without any luck. By early morning the winds blew consistently 30 to 35 knots with gusts near 45 knots. About 8 the next morning, we finally hooked an anchor on a crease in the rocky bottom. Two nights without any sleep and I was dead tired. Elaine stayed up in the cockpit and watched and made sure we didn't drag anchor and I laid down for a couple of hours.

The winds blew from 30 to 45-knots all day Sunday. Gordon was supposed to hit the Keys sometime tonight. I had an appointment to pull Jaibolero out on Monday morning and put him on the hard for a couple of months while we went back to Kentucky for the holidays. I finally raised someone at the marina on the radio about 2 PM and told him we had to have a slip or needed to be pulled out now. No one could survive the night in this anchorage with hurricane-force winds. I told him that our lives were in his hands. He said Jaibolero could not be lifted out in these winds but he would make room at the wall next to the lift for us to tie up for the night. This had its risks, but it was our only choice. We could have jumped in our dingy and left Jaibolero at anchor but this would have been the end for him, and we were without insurance.

We pulled anchors and headed in. I knew it would be a real challenge just to get Jaibolero tied up to the dock. The wind was blowing us away from the dock and I had about a foot clearance on each end to try to get him docked. When we stopped going forward, it wouldn't take but a few seconds for the winds to blow us up against the rocks on the other side of the canal. We would only have one chance to throw a bow line and a stern line--each of us throwing one to the two guys at the dock. I told Elaine our boat and our lives depended on her tossing a dock line at least fifteen feet into a forty knot wind. She looked petrified. I told her she could do it. She always comes through under pressure. She made a good toss. By the time I left the wheel, jumped out of the cockpit, and ran back to throw the stern line, I was so far away from the dock I didn't think I could possibly get the line there. The fellow caught the last six inches of line. He pulled the stern in a little and cleated the line. He went forward to help pull in the bow. They alternated, both at the stern and then at the bow, until they finally worked Jaibolero up next to the dock. I can't describe how relieved we were to be safely secured to the dock.

I started preparing Jaibolero for Gordon. I stripped everything off the top of him to reduce the windage and put out six dock lines on our starboard side. If the dock lines failed, Jaibolero would wash up on the rocks on the other side of the canal and he would be history.

We had no idea what to expect. This was not only our first hurricane but our first hurricane in a boat. We did everything we could think of to get ready, then we said our prayers. All we could do was wait and hope we didn't take a direct hit. I've spent my whole life chasing thrills but this was one thrill I could do without. I suggested a hurricane party for Gordon and spent the rest of the night apologizing. Needless to say, neither one of us slept a wink again that night. We saw 75 knot winds on our indicator and, at times, we heeled over about 35 to 40 degrees at the dock. We could hear gravel and trash banging into Jaibolero. It was miserable sitting down below not knowing if it was going to get worse. My third night in a row with very little sleep didn't help matters. It was very uncomfortable heeled over so far while tied up at the dock. The keel must have been up against the pilings which kept us from heeling over further. We just sat there looking at each other. It really was stupid staying on the boat that night. There was not a thing I could have done to save him if things had gotten worse. We should have been in a hurricane-proof building.

About daylight the winds backed down to about 30 knots and I opened the hatch and checked things out. The landscaping had taken a beating but none of the boats in the yard had blown over. Evidently, we didn't take a direct hit. Things could have been much worse. Things were a lot worse for the boats anchored at Gun Cay. We heard that only one survived. We were very lucky that we decided to sail on to Key Largo instead of staying at Gun Cay.

After the shakedown cruise I felt I had some real experience. Yes, I had made a few mistakes. I continued telling Elaine that a smart man learns from his mistakes and I was gaining wisdom at a phenomenal rate. I had also heard that adversity builds character. I doubt this but, if true, thanks to sailing, I should have one strong character. Seriously, I knew I must get my single side band (SSB) radio fixed or get another one. I would not attempt to go cruising again without weather reports. With a SSB we could get accurate weather reports anywhere. There were a couple of other things we needed for Jaibolero before we left on our circumnavigation of the Caribbean. We needed more batteries and a wind generator. But the single most important thing I needed to do during the next six weeks was to convince Elaine that I had this sailing thing figured out good enough so that I wouldn't get us killed.

Chapter 13

The Admiral Takes Over

The "sailing hillbillies" took off from Key Largo on January 26, 1995, heading for Venezuela. Since hurricanes rarely ever get as far south as Venezuela, we figured this is the place to be during the hurricane months from July to November. With our limited experience and our hillbilly luck, we needed to be as conservative as possible. Elaine was convinced that, if there was a tropical wave that turned into a hurricane, it would find us. We will look back on this decision as one that probably saved our lives, since 1995 will go in the books as one of the worst years ever for hurricanes. Every place that we considered staying during the hurricane months was devastated by hurricanes. Over 200 cruiser's lives were rumored to have been lost in Simpsons Bay on St. Martin and it was suppose to be a safe hurricane hole. No telling how many lives were lost on St. Thomas and the other Virgin Islands.

Since we had already cruised down to Georgetown on our shakedown cruise in the fall, we decided to take advantage of the good weather and get on down through the Exumas to Georgetown as quickly as possible. The weather kept us anchored in Georgetown for a week waiting for the right conditions to sail over to Rum Cay. Sailboats don't go into the wind very well, they like to go with the wind. Since the prevailing winds are the easterly to southeasterly trade winds, its a real challenge to get from Florida to the Virgin Islands and the Caribbean. You have to sail or motor into the wind and seas most of the time. During the winter months, northerns (cold fronts) move down through the Bahamas and the winds swing from the southeast, to south, to southwest, to west, and keep swinging around clockwise until it blows from the southeast again. Most of the time the cold fronts will move through in 24 to 36 hours. The game plan is to hop on one of these fronts and take advantage of the wind and let it blow you from one anchorage to another. Keep working your way toward the southeast by taking advantage of the fronts.

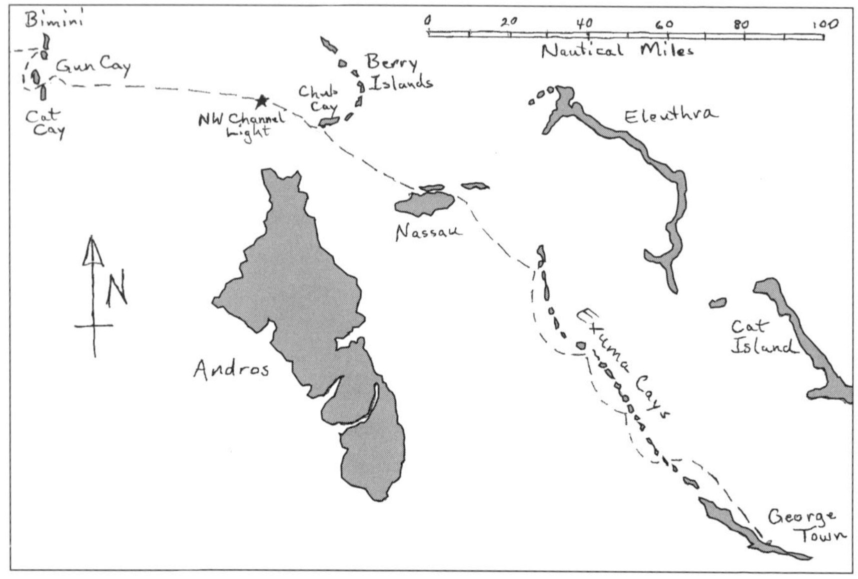

From Bimini to Georgetown

After a week the weatherman finally predicted a cold front to hit early the next morning with winds from the southwest in the 20-knot range. This was acceptable, so we went to town and stocked up on supplies. We awoke early, pulled anchor and took off. The cruising guide warned that the anchorage on Rum Cay is on a shelf exposed to south and west winds and seas. It is not surrounded by a reef that would protect it from offshore seas. In other words, the offshore seas hitting the shallow anchorage results in huge, steep waves very close together that will make anchoring very difficult. If the anchor holds, you would still suffer one horrendous beating until the wind changes around to the north. I never really thought much about this because the weatherman predicted the winds would be from the north by the time we got there.

We had to sail for about 35 miles just north of east to clear the reef at the northern tip of Long Island, then sail southeast for about 35 miles to get to Rum Cay. It should take about ten hours to make the trip. The sail from Long Island to Rum Cay is in open, deep water and with the wind against southeast swells, it makes for very large and rough seas. It was a very tiring and exhausting sail. My luck hadn't changed, it was still bad. We arrived late in the afternoon with winds between 20 and 25 knots still from the southwest. I raised the new little marina at Sumner Point on the radio. The dockmaster said there was no way to get us into the marina in these conditions. In good conditions they have to send someone out in a runabout to guide sailboats in through the coral heads. He told me we were going to have to stay out at sea or go into the anchorage and put out two anchors and hope the winds clock around pretty soon. We decided to try the anchoring.

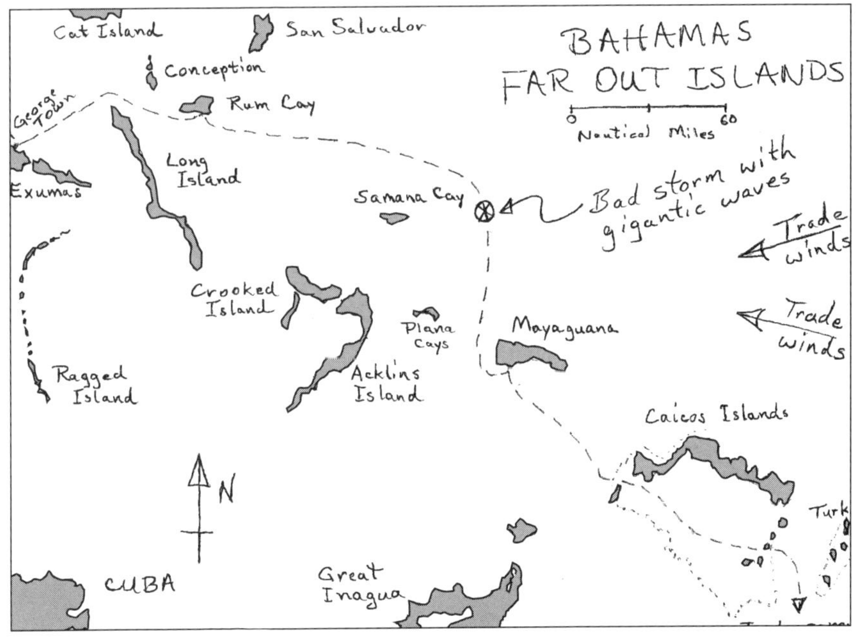

Georgetown to Luperon

There were at least 6 to 8-foot waves in the anchorage and they were very close together. We played the "try to get the anchors to hook" game. It was dangerous out on the bow in these conditions working with the anchors. It was all I could do to hold on and not be washed overboard. Jaibolero's bow was submarining through some of the waves. After about an hour of trying, I finally got the anchors to set. One moment Jaibolero would be pointed straight up in the air and the anchor rodes would be stretched to the point of breaking and the next second he was pointing straight down with waves breaking over the bow. We have a centerline aft berth and I looked back at Elaine trying to lay in bed. It was as if the bed was falling out from under her with every wave. I wanted to ask her if she was bored yet, but I didn't. My situation was precarious, at best. It definitely was not a time for joking. She gave up trying to lay down and went to the salon and just sat there not saying anything. Things had to get better. I told Elaine things couldn't get much worse. She just sat there in a trance. She knew better because, every time I said that, things got worse. Before the night was over we would see 40 to 45-knot winds still blowing from the southwest and 15 to 20-foot seas.

We discussed our options. We had two choices, neither good. We could stay at anchor and, if the anchors failed to hold or the tackle broke, we would probably be on the coral heads behind us before we could do anything. The other choice was to try to find our way out of the anchorage and back to sea. The cruising guide says to attempt this entrance or exit only in good conditions and in good light. We had neither. I thought we would have one chance in three of making it out safely. What's worse was I didn't think our chances at anchor were much better. We decided to stay put because our anchors were holding for the time being. My stomach was tied in knots. The cruising life was suppose to be good on a person's nerves. All it had done for me so far was to make my bad stomach worse.

I sat in the cockpit all night long waiting for the anchors to drag. I had to be ready to start the engine to keep us off the coral heads. Elaine would have to take the wheel while I pulled in the anchor rodes by hand. The ½ inch nylon snugger line on the chain anchor rode broke and the force of the waves was too much for the windlass. The one and a half inch solid, stainless shaft on the windlass bent almost straight forward, but it was still holding the anchor chain. We weren't the only ones in this predicament. There was a small sailboat about 200 yards to our right. This poor guy never did get his anchor to hold until the winds let up the next morning. He was out on the bow working in horrible conditions all night long.

We should have stayed out at sea and "hove-to" until the wind direction changed. We will never anchor again in an open anchorage with offshore winds of this magnitude. We could have "hove-to" on a starboard tack, battened down the hatches and had a reasonably comfortable night down below. I found out the next morning that the Danforth anchor had hooked on some coral and, by some miracle, it held. The winds clocked around about 10 AM the next morning. Things finally started to settle down and Elaine fixed us breakfast in silence. We ate in silence. I wasn't sure she would ever talk to me again. I tried to tell her this was the epitome of bad luck. The weatherman couldn't have picked a worse time to be wrong. Explaining this to Elaine rewarded me with that patented silent glare that I have learned to recognize as the look of total frustration. I told Elaine that you have to take a little bad with the good. She said it would take at least a hundred years of good to make up for last night.

Later on in the afternoon the marina sent someone out to guide us in through the coral heads. When Elaine stepped off onto the dock I thought that she would never step foot on a boat again. We had a welcoming committee waiting for us. The marina was small and only held about ten boats and everyone was on the dock. I got down on all fours and kissed the dock, trying to be funny, because everybody was watching. Men came up and shook my hand and women gave me a hug. We've never had a reception like this from total strangers before. It was obvious they were glad to see us alive. We all had a great happy hour with fresh lobster hors d'oeuvres. Everyone had "war stories" to tell and everyone agreed ours were the world champions. Somebody even suggested that we should write a book.

The single most enjoyable thing about cruising for us was the people we met. Most of them seem to have the key characteristics of successful managers or entrepreneurs. Not only are they good listeners, they are good communicators and they really seem to enjoy other people. It was fun meeting people and finding out what their story was before cruising and what their future plans were. Some of the cruisers were on sabbaticals and planned to return to work after a year or two but most were retired and planned on sailing for several years. If a boat that we haven't seen before pulls into the anchorage, we will dingy over and meet them and invite them to happy hour or whatever. Rarely have we ever pulled into an anchorage and not made some new friends before we left. The reunions were great too. It was fun pulling in and seeing friends again. There is hardly an anchorage that we come into nowadays that we don't know some of the cruisers.

Everything turns out for the best. Two good things happened at Rum Cay. The first, I learned a valuable lesson. One cruiser said that he always lets the Admiral (his wife) make the decision whether they go or not. That way it can never be his fault if things turn bad. From now on, I will, I repeat that I will always let Elaine make the decision whether we go or not. The second good thing that happened is that we became good friends with some cruisers at Rum Cay that we will never forget. I don't know if they were joking or not but one gal said they had a prayer vigil all night for us the night that we were anchored in Rum Cay. We have stayed in touch with and cruised off and on with these couples for the last two years--Tom and Ellie, Ann-Marie and Armond, and Jack and Jean. Anytime they get near a sandbar or a reef and things look a little shaky to them, they always say they will "do a Floyd" and just go for it!

After about a week the weatherman predicted a cold front but the Admirals all decided that the winds associated with it were a little too high. Luckily, another one followed the next day so the Captains were all given orders to prepare to sail. Four boats went out that afternoon headed for Mayaguana. Its a deep-water, overnight sail and it should have been a sleigh ride with the winds at our backs. I had every square inch of sail up and we got several miles ahead of the others. I wanted to show them this hillbilly could sail and that his boat was pretty fast. After all this talk about the Admirals deciding when to go, I was kind of hoping things wouldn't be so great so I could rub it in a little. I got my wish. That first cold front ran into a storm from the northeast and stalled waiting for us. When the cold front we were riding hit this stalled mess we were in for some real big, mixed-up seas.

About 1 AM, I looked back and there was a wave coming at us that looked way taller than Jaibolero's mast. I yelled below for Elaine to hold on that we were going for a ride. I switched the autopilot off and took the wheel. I had read about how you were suppose to steer on waves like this and now it was my chance to see if I remembered right. If we steered directly down the steep waves, the bow had a good chance of digging in and we would pitchpole (end over end)--which is the worst way to roll. If we steered at a 40 to 50-degree angle to the wave, we would be knocked down or round up into a broach and could roll over. By heading 20 degrees off the direction of the waves, we were supposed to have a better chance of not pitchpoling or rolling. That book must have been wrong or we needed a sea drogue to slow us down or something. Maybe the waves were just too big and steep. We were going so fast down this big wave that the rudder lost its affect and Jaibolero broached, turned to port and laid over on his side. I thought we were going to do a complete 360 degree roll. By now, I only had about half of the head-sail out and no mainsail. I was scrambling to hold on. I should have had my safety harness on but I didn't. I think the mast hit the water. I couldn't really tell because I couldn't see through the Bimini. All the ports and hatches were closed so we couldn't take on any water and I knew Jaibolero's 9000 pound keel would straighten us back up. When he straightened up I jumped outside the cockpit and rolled in more of the headsail until there was just a patch left out. I yelled down to Elaine to hand me my safety harness.

It was really crazy because, for several minutes, everything would be going fine and all of a sudden one of those giant waves would come up behind us and, no matter what I did, Jaibolero would broach. I really couldn't tell how tall the waves were, but everything I have read says they are about one half as big as they look. They looked much taller than the mast, which was 54 feet, so the waves must have been at least 30 to 40 feet. The largest ones could have been 50 to 60 feet; these were the ones that caused us to broach four times before things finally let up. I tried something a little different each time and we still broached. I wanted to put out the drogue or some warps, but I was afraid to leave the cockpit and let the autopilot steer Jaibolero in these conditions.

The other boats experienced some large waves but nothing like we did. They did not sail as far to the east as we did before the bad weather hit. We were at such a good point of sail and were making such good time that I decided to sail at least 30 miles further east before turning south. This way we would still have a favorable wind to sail on down to Mayaguana, even if the front passed us and the winds clocked around to the east. My transmission had slipped a little a couple of times, and I didn't want to use it if I didn't have to. As

I told the Admiral, sometimes you can make all the right decisions and they turn out wrong. That is sailing.

The seas calmed down some the next day and we found a calm anchorage on the south side of Mayaguana. We saw one of the most beautiful sunsets we had ever seen. We had a nice sail down to the Caicos and could have stayed for weeks, but we were kind of pressed for time. Some family was to meet us in the Virgin Islands for spring break on March the tenth. It was a long way to go with a weak transmission.

Chapter 14

Dominican Republic to Puerto Rico

The Admiral caught a good weather window and we had a beautiful overnight sail down to Luperon on the north side of the Dominican Republic. The bay at Luperon was well protected and calm as a duck's pond. This was our first experience with a third-world country. Getting checked in through customs was a real experience. A clearance party of five men rowed out to our boat with guns and boarded us. We had been warned that they would ask for beer and aspirin. Needless to say, no one in their right mind was going to refuse a few aspirin to a fellow with a gun. I showed them Jaibolero's papers and they all nodded their heads and asked for cervezas (beer). It was quite obvious they wanted to celebrate our good fortune in arriving at Luperon.

Luperon was a typical small fishing village that was trying to take advantage of a tourist boom that hadn't happened yet. There was one road through town. There were guards with machine guns at each end of town. Cows, chickens and donkeys roamed up and down the dirt streets. The homes were built right on the street and most did not have windows or doors and they all appeared to have dirt floors. While walking along the street, we could see right inside. They were immaculate considering the conditions. The most amazing thing was how clean and neat all the young ones were in their little uniforms as they went to school. They were a handsome and friendly race. The restaurants were clean and served great food. We were having lunch at a restaurant while a cattle drive was being held right down the middle of the main street. Two other couples and the Admiral and I hired a minibus and went inland on a sight-seeing trip to Santiago. This was the highlight of our cruise thus far.

The Dominican Republic was beautiful and the people were gracious except for the young hard-nosed commandante in Puerto Plata. We were motorsailing east along the coast when my transmission started slipping and the winds started picking up, so we decided to stop at Puerto Plata and wait for better conditions. Puerto Plata was a major port and commercial center and most cruisers bypass it because the water was dirty and oily and the town was filthy. We only stayed for one day and went to customs to check out. For some reason the commandante didn't like my looks and followed us back to Jaibolero for a search. I had a small handgun that I never claimed at customs, it was kept well hidden on board. I figured I would never get searched. If this commandante had found my pistol, he would have confiscated our boat and put us in jail--probably the worse jail in the world. All kinds of horrible thoughts were running through my mind. I could picture Elaine and I in a third-world jail. Even if I survived the jail, she would kill me. The commandante was a real pro at searching boats. Every place I had considered hiding the gun, he searched. The gun was a hammerless 38 special. I had it in my right jogging shoe with a dirty sock on top of it. The shoes were on a shelf beside the aft birth where we slept. Elaine complained several times about those stinking shoes. My thinking was, the more they stunk, the less likely anyone would want to touch them and thus find the gun. The commandante tore Jaibolero apart but he never found it, thank God. The 30 minutes he was on board may be the worst 30 minutes of my life. The sail out of Puerto Plata Harbor was one of the happiest moments of my life. Words cannot describe how I felt as Puerto Plata went out of sight.

We did an overnighter to get around to Samana. Samana was the last stop before crossing the Mona Passage over to Puerto Rico. People come from all over the world to Samana in February and March to see the sperm whales during mating season. It was big business for the resorts around Samana and for the whale-watching boats. It was a beautiful sight to see them leap up out of the water and land with a big splash. I told Elaine I figured out why they jump out of the water the way they do. These poor whales swim thousands of miles to come down here every year for a vacation and a little "hanky panky." No wonder they get upset and jump around. They can't have any privacy with all these boats full of tourists trying to watch them!

Samana was beautiful but a cold front was passing through, so we pulled anchor and headed for Boqueron, Puerto Rico. We had just made it out of the harbor when the transmission went out completely. We had to sail across the dreaded Mona Passage. It was suppose to be the worse crossing we would face because it usually has high winds and seas. I told Elaine it was no big deal, that we were a sailboat, we shouldn't need a transmission. We would just sail to Boqueron. No one has ever heard of a dead calm in the Mona Passage but, we found one, and with no transmission. More hillbilly luck. We just sat there floating like a cork. There wasn't as much as a ripple on the water. For six hours the sails just hung loose and we turned in circles. Finally, late in the afternoon, a storm blew in from the northeast and we made it into Boqueron Bay about 10 PM that night. Navigating under power into Boqueron Bay in daylight and good weather conditions would be a challenge. I was not looking forward to sailing in and dropping anchor under sail in the dark in a strange anchorage. This was borderline insanity. We were lucky that the winds held up. We were in the middle of the bay cautiously sailing along under mainsail and all of a sudden we hit something submerged and it sounded bad. I looked at the depth meter and we were in fairly deep water and the charts don't show a thing. I jumped down below and raised up the floor boards and checked the bilges. We weren't sinking so I continued on in and dropped anchor. The next morning I dove on the keel and there was a huge gouge down the side of the keel. I talked to several locals and they all said there was nothing out there to hit. I know better. I told Elaine it must have been a submarine.

It only took one day to get a shop manual and a transmission rebuild kit flown in from the States. There was one man who all the cruisers went to for mechanical repairs. He spoke a little English and he would set cruisers up with the right person to repair whatever was broken. For three days in a row he made appointments with three different mechanics. Each one looked at the manual and started to shake their head. Finally he said that was it, nobody would rebuild my transmission. To get from the west end of Puerto Rico to the east end usually takes at least a week of motoring into heavy winds and seas. Sailing would be almost impossible. I had to get the transmission fixed and fast, if we were going to make it to Fajardo to pick the kids up for spring break.

With my experience building racing motorcycles through the years, I knew I could rebuild the transmission if I had a decent place to work. I asked the interpreter to just find me some place I could work that had a vise, an air compressor and a hydraulic press. He knew just the place. He would arrange it and pick me up in the morning and take me there. I pulled the transmission out that night, got my tools ready and studied the manual. This idiot took me to a Puerto Rican "Hells' Angels" hangout. There were choppers everywhere. Most of them not running. There was a 40's model house trailer with a lean-to that had a sheet of metal for a roof over a bench with a vise. He did have an air compressor. I had to give him $40 to work here for the day. I asked where the hydraulic press was and the interpreter said it was just down the road at this guy's brother's shop. What choice did I have?

I disassembled the transmission and inspected all the bearings, thrust washers and spacers and had everything all cleaned up and in the perfect order to go back together. All I needed to do was press the bearings off the main shaft, replace the clutch plates and press the bearings back on. I used sign language to get this guy to take me to his brother's place. He motioned for me to follow him. We had to walk two blocks to borrow a truck. Nobody was home. I don't remember this guys name but I'm going to call him Jose. Well, Jose started throwing a fit. He looked in the ash tray, under the seat, and under the floor mats and there were no keys. I guess it was my fault because I looked at him in such disgust that Jose starting pulling wires out from under the dash and cutting them with his knife. He hot wired the truck. The battery was dead. My first thought was, thank God we're not stealing the truck. I could see the headlines back home, "Local man killed while in jail in Puerto Rico for stealing $50 truck." Jose was screaming and beating on the steering wheel when a car pulled up with two women and about a dozen kids. Jose knew them and they had jumper cables. We jumped the battery and stole the truck.

Jose's brother's place was about 20 miles away in the next little community. About half way there the sky began to turn black and the wind started blowing. The rain started pouring and the wind was blowing on my side of the truck. I tried rolling my window up and found out there was no glass. I wasn't about to scoot over next to Jose to stay dry so I just sat there and got soaked. Jose was having a big laugh about something when the engine started missing. He started beating on the dash while looking at the instruments. It was obvious we were running out of gas in the middle of nowhere, in a stolen truck, in a horrible rain storm. Jose jumped out of the truck, slammed the door, kicked it a couple of times and took off walking in the rain storm. He wasn't about to leave me alone in a stolen truck on the side of the road. I put the transmission shaft on the hump to try and keep it dry and took off after him. I just knew it would be ten miles to the next service station. We were lucky. It was only about a mile away. I paid for a couple of gallons of gas and the next car that came in took us back to the truck. We finally made it to the shop to use the hydraulic press. The way things were going I figured the press would be broken or something but, that wasn't the problem. The problem was Jose owed his brother some money and we weren't going anywhere near his shop. They cussed and spit on each other. I knew how to fix this so I pulled out a $20 bill and walked up between them and gave the brother the twenty. He took the twenty, and stuck it in his pocket and went back to cussing Jose. This was it, I was going to use this press or die trying. I walked into the shop past two guys who put their arms up to stop me. I stopped and said a few words to them. They couldn't understand a word I was saying but they could see I was serious. I went in and found the press but could not find the bearing holders I needed. The shop owner came in and ended up being very helpful. I replaced the clutch plates and pressed the bearings back on. I shook the man's hand and left.

We made it back to Jose's place. It had almost quit raining. Just when I thought things couldn't get any worse, they did. The lean-to roof had fallen down from the storm. All the bearings and everything on the bench were standing in water. I was hunting for a dry place to put down the main shaft when I looked up and this idiot had pushed all of the shims, spacers, bearings and other parts all together in a pile at one end of the bench. He was trying to wipe the water off with his other hand. Everything was totally mixed up. It was going to be impossible to put the transmission back together without end calipers, dial indicators, feeler gauges, etc., and we didn't have them. About then, he realized what he had done. I was past the point of a nervous breakdown. If looks could kill, he would be dead and he knew it. He backed away and went inside his trailer and started screaming at some woman. She screamed back a few times. In a few minutes he came out with two big beers and a joint rolled up like a cigar. I passed on the joint but not the beer.

Hurth transmissions require just the right clearances to operate and last very long. It took me several tries to get it back together to the point where the three shafts all turned freely without much end play. I didn't have any of the right tools, so I had to put the transmission together and test it by feel. I installed it in the boat. I told Elaine there was a very slim chance of it working and that, if it did work, it couldn't last long. I was wrong, but this time being wrong was right. It not only got us to the Virgin Islands but all the way down to Venezuela without slipping before I took it back to the States to have the factory representatives go through it.

Chapter 15

Bad Year for Hurricanes

The trip from Boqueron along the south coast of Puerto Rico to Fajardo on the east end was the hardest part of the whole cruise from Florida to South America. The trade winds from the southeast build choppy 6 to 8-foot seas that will stop a sailboat. Beating into these type seas was known as the "Caribbean Two-Step;" two steps forward, one step back. Sometimes, it was one step forward and two steps back. There was only one sensible way to do it and that was to take advantage of the night-time conditions. Late at night there was usually a slight off-shore breeze close to shore caused by the cooling of the land. This calmed the seas close to shore until about 9 AM the next morning. We would leave the anchorage at 3 AM or 4 AM and motorsail close to shore to get our easting and tuck into the next anchorage before the seas started building up. Then, take the rest of the day to sight see and go to bed early.

We made four stops along the south coast of Puerto Rico. Some cruisers make as many as eleven stops, but we were pressed for time. We were really concerned about the transmission holding up. If it

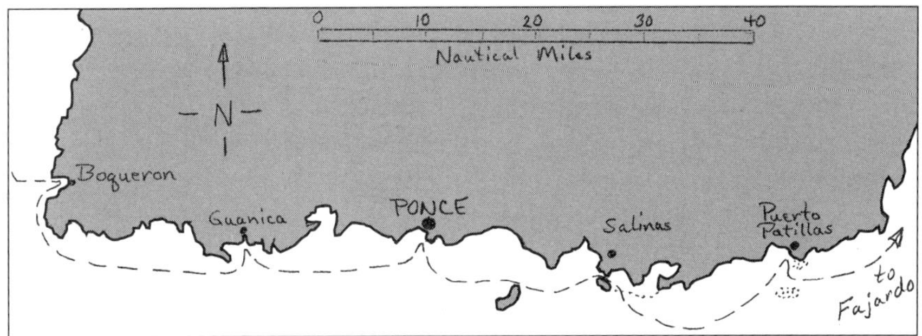

The south coast of Puerto Rico

failed, we would have a marathon sail around the clock for several days beating into steep waves to get to Fajardo. Another major concern was pulling anchor in the dark and maneuvering out of strange anchorages without hitting something or running aground. But the most frightening thing was tacking back and forth right next to shore in total darkness without radar. It sounds crazy but that's the way it has to be done. The day we dropped anchor off Fajardo, I felt like the ant that had moved the rubber tree plant. The kids were flying to San Juan in two days and we had just enough time to rent a car and stock the boat up again. We were only a one day sail from the Virgin Islands. We had arrived!!!!

We picked up our son Brian and his wife, Kirsten, and Jason and his friend, Lisa, at the airport. By the time we reached Fajardo a nasty front had hit and it was raining "cats and dogs." The wind had whipped up some mean seas. I told everyone we were in for a wet and rough dingy ride. The anchorage at Fajardo was about a mile off shore at Isleta Marina. There was a bay at Fajardo but it was open to east and northeast winds, a very poor anchorage. The anchorage at Isleta Marina was protected fairly well from all wind directions but it was a long dingy ride away, especially in these conditions. We would have to make two trips. I told everyone that they could get motel rooms if they wanted, but I had to go back to the boat to make sure the anchor wasn't dragging. I expected the boys to be macho but the girls spoke up and said they were game if I was. The plan was to take the women first and bring back some big garbage bags to keep the luggage dry. I would bring the boys and the luggage on the second trip.

We had left the dingy tied up in a protected marina and we really couldn't tell how bad it was out in the bay. The winds were out of the northeast and blowing right into the bay. The waves were a lot worse than I thought. We were soaked before we cleared the entrance to the marina. It would have been impossible for me to have made it by myself. The wind would have blown the dingy over backwards on the first big wave. Kirsten and Lisa, up front in the dingy, helped hold it down. The wind was blowing the tops off the waves. I could hardly see for the salt water in my eyes. We were rounding the point out of Fajardo Bay when Kirsten screamed that something was sticking out of the water right in front of us. I realized we were too close to shore and it must be coral. If the coral hits the dingy we were done for. I turned the dingy and headed for deeper waters. Kirsten said we missed it by inches. I finally got the girls to Jaibolero and headed back for the boys. They were upset and wanted to know what took me so long. I told them to hop in and they would find out. The garbage bags helped keep the luggage dry but we were soaked to the bone by the time we made it to Jaibolero.

The weather had settled down a little the next morning but it was still pretty nasty, too bad for us to sail to St. Thomas. The weather forecast little change for the next few days. In other words, we were stuck in Fajardo. I told the kids there was plenty to see around Fajardo. We could go to Isla Palomino which was only a few miles away and it had super beaches. No one wanted to hear this. The boys accused me of loosing my nerve. They said I was getting soft in my old age. They all agreed that a tough day sail would be fun and it wasn't but thirty miles to St. Thomas. I looked at the Admiral and she shook her head no. The boys and Kirsten were pleading. The Admiral finally gave in. I told everyone to put everything up and batten down the hatches because we were going to "do a Floyd" and go for it. A loud cheer erupted. Elaine handed out the dramamine. I pulled anchor and we took off. I had a deep reef in the mainsail and the headsail. We were doing max hull speed pinching the wind. Jaibolero was going to be tested. Kirsten stood on the windward side holding on to the shrouds with spray from the salt water soaking her as we burst through the waves. Her hair was blowing straight back. She would yell with joy every time we hit a big wave. If she was trying to impress me, it was working. She said she was born for this. Lisa looked like she wished she had never been born. She was green and had the dry heaves. I wasn't feeling up to par myself. I was beginning to wish I had taken a dramamine.

We were really hauling the mail about eight miles from St. Thomas when I heard this loud noise and the main began flying free. The outhaul, the line (sheet) that keeps the mainsail pulled back tight, broke and the mainsail was dangerous as it snapped back and forth. I started the engine and turned on the autopilot. We were lucky the roller furling didn't fail in these conditions. I was able to roll in the main and continue on with the headsail and the engine. We dropped anchor at Charlotte Amalie on St. Thomas. Our guests couldn't wait to get cleaned up and check out the night life. Elaine and I couldn't wait to eat and hit the sack. Our age was showing.

Our week with the kids was one of the best times of our lives. We sailed over to St. Johns. We snorkeled, wind surfed, shopped and did some sight-seeing. The kids did the night life every night. We sailed back over to Fajardo to take the kids back to the airport. While we were there, we met a boat insurance agent who finally arranged for us to purchase insurance through an agent in Florida. Every insurance company that I could find turned us down before we left the States. Looking back on things, I can't blame them. I wouldn't insure me either. Now that we had successfully made it to the Virgin Islands they figured we must know something. Anyway, we arranged for a survey and got the insurance. Just one catch, for hurricane season we had to be below latitude 15 by August 1 or our insurance wouldn't pay off. We now look back on this policy as probably saving our lives, because we decided to keep the policy and head down through the Leewards and Windwards in order to spend most of hurricane season in the Grenadines and Trinidad.

The sail from the British Virgins over to St. Martin was an overnight beat into the wind but it was worth it. We loved the restaurants and Elaine loved the shopping on St. Martin. The French pastries and the ice cream parlors were enough to keep Elaine here forever. Each island we visited had its own character and history. St. Barthelemy was clean and modern with beautiful architecture and lovely landscaping. We were sure glad we saw these two places when we did because Hurricane Luis wiped them out later in the year. Simpsons Bay on St. Martin was suppose to be a good hurricane hole for cruisers, but Luis proved this to be false. The Virgins were devastated by Hurricane Marilyn. 1995 was a bad year for hurricanes.

We visited most of the islands in the Leewards and Windwards as we made our way south. We especially loved Trafalgar Falls on Dominica, Fort Napoleon on Isle des Saintes, The Pitons on St. Lucia, Port Elizabeth on Bequia, Ft. Orange on St. Eustatius, the Soufriere and the Great Alps Waterfall on Montserrat, the Tobago Cays in the

A FUN CREW -
Honey, Barb, Pam, Lynn (in taxi), Dan, Gail, Janie (in taxi), Walt, Elaine, Lou, Floyd

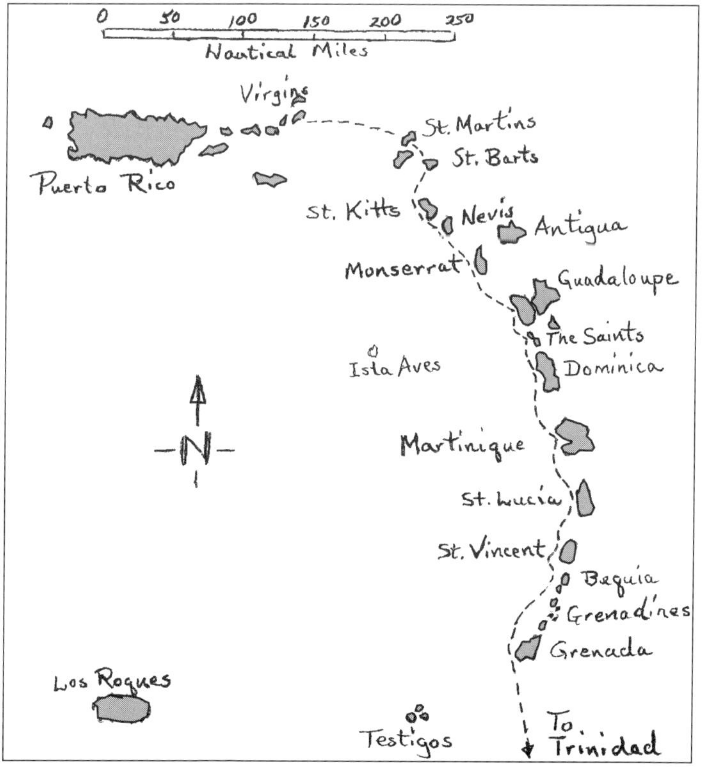

The Windward and Leeward Islands of the Caribbean.

Happy hour on Jaibolero.

Grenadines and the River Deshaies on Guadeloupe. Each island has its own character and history. There were always some fellow cruisers ready to hire a van and do a tour. The more, the merrier. Happy hour was always special. Sometimes we would have a special place to go but most of the time everybody would meet on a boat and swap stories.

Our favorite anchorage down through the island chain was the Tobago Cays in the Southern Grenadines. The Tobago Cays were made up of four small islands protected by a horseshoe reef. The anchorage used by most of the cruisers was right up behind the reef facing the trade winds. There was always a fantastic breeze and the wind generators worked great. In fact, it was the only place we had found where we had to be wasteful with the electricity to keep from overcharging the batteries. The wind generator and solar panels would supply enough power for most cruisers to run their watermaker, refrigeration, etc. without having to run their engine. They never had to leave for supplies, the boat boys would deliver supplies from Union or Mayreau. The boat boys would always have fresh fish and lobster for those like me who would rather buy than fish or dive.

The snorkeling on Horseshoe Reef was superb. In fact, it was the best I've seen in the Leeward or Windward Islands. The reef colors were a kaleidoscope of gold, brown, blue, turquoise, and green. There were beautiful palm trees lining the beaches where we built bonfires and had happy hours or potlucks. Each clear night we would sit late in the cockpit and enjoy the stars. They seemed more abundant and brighter than ever before. We talked to one cruiser who had been around the world. He claimed the Tobago Cays was at the top of his list.

It was only two miles from the anchorage on Tobago Cays to Salt Whistle Bay on Mayreau. We would take Jaibolero over there for the night, make our phone calls and have dinner out with some friends. The only exercise we'd had for over a week was snorkeling so I was excited about getting in a good jog. There was a nice little resort at Salt Whistle Bay but the main village was about a half a mile away. To get there we had to follow this steep, rocky trail up over a hill and back down to the village. Elaine walked and I jogged. I would jog a ways up the trail and back down to Elaine to make sure she was alright and I would jog back up again. I had jogged a pretty good distance up the hill when I noticed off to the left some Texas longhorn cattle roaming free. I went back and told Elaine she wasn't going to believe it but there were longhorn cattle up the hill. She looked at me and stopped. She said she wasn't going anywhere near some wild cattle. I told her she was being silly, that those cattle were like pets or they wouldn't be roaming free. Boy, was I ever wrong.

Elaine made me walk beside her up to where the cattle were. I just had to show her how tame these cattle were. Against some intense protesting, I walked down to where the bull and his three heifers were eating on some kind of a bush. I had never seen horns on cattle like these before. I really wanted to pet this bull. As I slowly approached him, he turned and faced me. He looked friendly. I was talking to him nice and easy and told him I just wanted to scratch his head a little. As I reached out my hand, he lowered his head and shook it back and forth. Then he started to paw the ground and I realized I had failed to make a friend. I started slowly back away from him while talking softly. Everything was fine until I turned around and here he came. I screamed for Elaine to climb a tree. My Nike's were throwing some gravel. I couldn't go up to the trail because the bull might turn on Elaine. I jumped behind a tree and started waving my arms and the bull came charging the tree. If he started one way, I went the other. I made sure and kept the tree between the bull and me. He couldn't get to me. After a few minutes, he meandered back down to his heifers. Elaine yelled down and asked if I was alright. I went back up the trail and found her. She was very upset and said that was the dumbest thing she had ever seen me do. I told her that bull was lucky, I was getting ready to pick up a stick and wear his hide out. That she didn't know it, but I had probably saved her life by keeping the bull chasing me around the tree and this is the kind of thanks I get. I faked one of my "hurt feelings" episodes but couldn't get any sympathy.

She made sure that I was not going to get one foot away from her after that. A little further up the hill there was a little trail off to the right and I could see some tombstones. I love looking around old graveyards so we headed down that path. As we approached the graveyard I noticed an old donkey up in front of us. Donkeys are usually friendly and harmless so I didn't think much about him. We were looking at some head stones and, the next thing I know, this donkey starts charging us, he-hawing loudly, with his mouth wide open and showing these huge teeth. I knew we couldn't outrun a donkey and there wasn't but one thing to do, stand there and fight. I reached down and picked up two large, baseball-sized rocks. I cut loose with the first one and made the pitch of a lifetime. It hit him square on the nose. He stopped in his tracks about ten feet in front of me. I almost felt sorry for him for an instant, but this donkey needed to learn a lesson. I reared back and threw the other rock and hit him on the shoulder as he turned around to run up in the bushes. I picked up a couple more rocks and we headed back to the main trail.

We finally made it over the hill and down to the village. As we started into the village, Elaine went over to this neat little old church and started peeking in the windows. I started jogging again as the rock path turned into a paved road. There were two mangy island dogs, they all look alike, laying next to the road as I approached them. I don't know what I did wrong but they started howling and attacking me. I started raising my legs up and down real fast, waving my arms around, and screaming at them in hopes of scaring them away. Within seconds, every dog in the village (and there was a bunch), had circled me and were howling and snapping at my legs. This was the most frightened I think I have ever been. Elaine was screaming for someone to help. Finally, two old ladies came with brooms and ran the dogs off. I was standing there shaking with my heart about to jump out of my chest. One of the old ladies looked at me and said, "Don't run, white man, don't run." They turned around and went back to their homes swatting at dogs on the way.

On the way back over the hill to the anchorage I found a nice piece of wood for a weapon. We didn't know what was going to attack us next. I told Elaine that the animals on this island were crazy. This whole day was like a chapter out of a Stephen King novel. Elaine said I started it all by teasing the bull. I asked her if she thought that bull told the donkey and the dogs to attack me. She said it could be. I did think something was really weird about this place.

We sailed back up to St. Lucia and left Jaibolero at Rodney Bay Marina and flew home for the month of August. Rodney Bay was a well-protected bay and a good safe place to leave a boat. Some friends of ours stayed on Jaibolero while having work done on their boat. They had to get Jaibolero ready for two hurricanes while we were gone. Both hurricanes just missed St. Lucia. We were only back in St. Lucia for two days when the weather forecasters predicted that Hurricane Marilyn was going to hit St. Lucia dead center. We were anchored out and were prepared to head south but decided against going to sea with a hurricane breathing down our necks. We went back into the marina and tied Jaibolero off with twelve dock lines. It was a solemn feeling on the docks as everyone got prepared by stripping everything off the top of their boats trying to reduce windage. Two other hurricanes had just missed and this one was going to be the big lick. A direct hit and Jaibolero and all the other boats were history. The Admiral decided that we would not stay on the boat when Marilyn got close. I told her the Captain always goes down with the ship. She knew me better than that. She sent me out to find as safe a place as possible to go when the time came.

Marilyn was only 50 miles to the east of St. Lucia when she stopped and built up strength. A boat charter business at the marina was getting satellite pictures every few minutes and it looked like a time for prayers. After a while, Marilyn started moving again but started heading more north. St. Lucia was spared but the Virgin Islands were going to get Marilyn's wrath and fury. St. Thomas would be devastated. It was time to get further south.

We put Jaibolero back in sailing condition, cleaned the bottom, prop and provisioned. The seas finally started to settle down after a couple of days but there was another darn tropical wave heading toward the Windward Islands. This "dodge the hurricane" game was not fun. We needed a lattitude adjustment to get out of the hurricane belt. It was decision time again. We could go back into Rodney Bay Marina, wait until it passed and hope for a better window (which seemed unlikely), or bite the bullet and go for it. Marilyn had just missed us but the next one might not pass by us. It looked like the tropical wave would hit us somewhere around Grenada if we headed south. If it didn't upgrade to a storm or hurricane, it wouldn't be too bad. The Admiral accused me of needing something to write about. We finally decided to sail down to Bequia and then evaluate things.

We stayed the night on anchor at Bequia. The tropical wave that was headed for Grenada had conditions favorable for an upgrade but it hadn't happened yet. It was at least 150 miles from Bequia to Trinidad with a two knot current to contend with. After a couple hours of evaluating the go or no-go decision, the Admiral finally gave the order to prepare to sail--to "do a Floyd" and go for it.. We left Bequia about 10 AM and were going to sail straight through without stopping at Grenada. Even with a reefed main and headsail we made maximum hull speed all day long. These were not ideal conditions but we were going south fast. I predicted the tropical wave would hit us just north of Grenada, and it did. We could see it coming from a long way off. The sky was black and the lightning was frightening. It was gut check time. I shortened sails even more, got out the safety harnesses and started going over in my mind the things I had to do if lightning hit us.

The wind and seas were not my worry. I felt we could survive them. It was the lightning. All of a sudden all hell broke loose. The lightning flashes were coming fast and furious and the wind was screaming through the shrouds. The lightning was hitting so close that it was shaking the boat. My electronics were going crazy. I expected a lightning bolt to hit the mast and blow a hole in the boat at any time. Elaine was giving me that "deer in the headlight" look that I hadn't seen for a while. There is nothing any more agonizing than just sitting there feeling totally helpless.

The storm finally passed and my electronics settled back down. It was getting dark as we sailed past Grenada and we decided to sail on through the night to Trinidad. We had three more squalls (spinoff from the tropical wave) hit us before the night was over. I asked Elaine why the worse year ever for hurricanes has to be the year we go cruising? She said I got what I wanted, another chapter to write. She accused me of risking our lives so I would have something to write about. I reminded her that we made this decision together and she was as much at fault as me. After all she was the Admiral and the Admiral has the final say so. She said I knew how bad it was going to be and didn't give her the true facts.

We sailed into Trinidad about 2 PM the next day, September 20. Jaibolero and I were her heroes again. We got her to Trinidad so she could go shopping with all her friends, redecorate the boat and pump up Trinidad's economy. We were with several friends that afternoon at happy hour at the yacht club. One of them asked me if I had known that there was a tropical storm predicted to hit Grenada the previous afternoon at about the same time as we had sailed past. I said, "I wasn't about to let a little tropical storm keep us from having happy hour with our friends today. It wasn't so bad, we had sailed through worse." Elaine spoke up and described what we had experienced. I said, "I am a new man, no more crazy stuff for me. I have learned my lesson." Elaine said, "If anyone here believes that, please stand up." One guy almost stood up but he shook his head and sat back down. Everybody had a big laugh.

Chapter 16

Venezuela

On October 1 we decided to sail over to Venezuela. On the way we anchored a couple of nights at Cabo San Francisco on the Peninsula De Paria. It was famous among the cruisers for the monkeys that came down to the berry trees next to the water at dawn and had breakfast each morning. We took a thermos of coffee and floated in the dingy right under them. We especially liked watching the mothers with the little ones on their backs. Our next stop was Los Testigos. This place is a "10" on everybody's scale. I snorkeled off the back of the boat and got two big lobsters for supper. I climbed some sand dunes and walked on one of the most beautiful beaches in the world. The only other foot prints I saw belonged to some birds and a little lizard. The Guardia Nacional would only let cruisers stay a couple of days without clearing in through Venezuela customs and that has to be done on the mainland or at Isla Margarita.

We had a great downwind sail over to Margarita so we could clear in through customs. Margarita was very cruiser friendly. Most sources refer to it as South America's top resort island. Everything was duty free on Margarita and people come there from everywhere to shop. The favorable exchange for U.S. dollars made for even better bargains. The premium beer there was Polar beer--about $3 a case. Ice cold beer on the beach was 60 Bolivars which was about 20 cents. I liked this place. Almost every prescription was about ten percent of its cost in the U.S. and by the same pharmaceutical companies. Diesel fuel was about 5 cents a gallon. No wonder the anchorage always had a couple hundred boats.

I never thought it would ever happen, Elaine finally got tired of shopping, so we pulled anchor and headed for Puerto La Cruz, the boating capitol of Venezuela. We stayed at Bahia Redondo Marina in Puerto La Cruz. There was obviously a lot of money in this area, especially in the El Morro area where the marinas were located. There were still some very poor areas in Puerto La Cruz but, for the most part, the people were very nice and helpful. The economy was very cruiser friendly. A cruiser could get almost anything he needed locally and special items could be shipped from the U.S. in a couple of days. The attractive exchange rates and very low labor rates of about $10 per day was just too good for most cruisers to pass up. I had a complete bottom job done on Jaibolero for about one third of the cost in the U.S.

The local market was two blocks from the marina. We could buy enough fresh vegetables, fruit, fish, shrimp, etc. for us for a week for about $10 U.S. Almost everyone stayed the full six months their Visa allowed. Many would leave for the required three months and return for six more months. We did.

Many of the cruisers did inland trips. We rented a car for a week with another couple, Tom and Ellie, and drove up in the Andes to Merida. It was a blast. I drove hard for two days to get there. We went through Caracas and were amazed that most of the people lived in block houses with no windows and tin roofs. We were told that some areas don't even have water or electricity, much less sewers in their homes. There were waterspouts, one for about every 50 families. We stopped to take some pictures and met two future Venezuelan beauty queens. They stole our hearts. Like kids everywhere they loved having their picture taken. They were very friendly and seemed very happy.

Future beauty queens, kids are great everywhere.

Our next stop was Colonia Tovar, a totally German community, just a couple hours drive from Caracas. We were told no one but full-blooded Germans could own land in this area. I'm sure a lot of Hitler's people and their descendants lived here and controlled this area. The city and all the homes for miles around looked like they belonged in Germany, not in Venezuela.

Colonia Tovar

We were driving through Valencia about 9 PM looking for a place to stay the night. We had stopped and inspected a couple of motels and had seen cockroaches so big that a half dozen of them could carry a small child away. We were driving along and Elaine said we just passed a place that looked like it belonged in Disneyworld. I turned around and we drove in through a huge archway up to a booth like we were entering a drive-in theater. Ellie could speak a little Spanish but she couldn't understand the woman in the booth. We finally figured out the price and paid her. It was something like six dollars U.S. She gave us a key. I held up two fingers and pointed at the key. She gave us another key and I drove on in. Elaine said the woman was shaking her head as we drove off.

The whole compound had walls about 12 feet tall with razor wire on top of the walls. We found our rooms. Each one was up over a garage. We felt safe because there were a couple of guards walking around with machine guns. The rooms were something else. There was red velvet and black vinyl everywhere. They were absolutely spotless, no blankets or bedspreads, just snow white sheets. Elaine jumped in the bathroom real quick and I heard her say the bathroom was really clean. I sat down on the bed and, it didn't make any difference which way I looked, I could see myself. Mirrors were everywhere. Elaine came out of the bathroom and looked around and then saw me grinning like a possum. She said her favorite expression, "Oh, my God." I told her we even had a TV and flipped it on. I started flipping channels, the same "xxx" stuff was on every channel. I told her this place was sure no Disneyland. We went next door to Tom and Ellie's room and it was the same way. I told them I wasn't for sure but I think we had only rented this place for an hour and we were suppose to have just one room. We all had a big laugh. Elaine and Ellie wanted to leave but Tom and I protested. This place was clean and safe and we were staying here. Elaine and I went back to our room just as room service was bringing us our complimentary rum and coke. Elaine wouldn't let me watch TV so we went to bed early.

The next morning driving down the road we had a good laugh about the night before. I told the girls we would probably be in the movies next week. Elaine and Ellie looked at each other and simultaneously said, "Oh, my God."

Typical road in the Andes, no guard rails.

On the way to Merida we got as high as 16,000 feet--the roads were treacherous. We stayed at the Monks Inn on the way there. It was a Monastery/Inn built about 1630 as a safe place for businessmen to stay on their way to Merida to trade or purchase goods. It was the neatest place we had ever stayed.

Los Frailes (Monks Inn), most charming.

Castillo San Ignacio in Mucuchies, looks like medieval Europe.

The next morning we were driving towards Merida when we saw what looked like a castle. We stopped to check it out. It was not open yet and the parking lot was not paved but we went in anyway. It was the Castillo San Ignacio. The manager showed us around and it was phenomenal. I went to use the bathroom and have never seen one more exquisite. The masonry and wood work was something you would have to see to believe. The lobby was huge and all the woodwork and ceiling was massive teak. Beams divided the ceiling into panels about two feet by three feet. Their regular clients could have their coat of arms painted in these panels.

In Merida we stayed at a quaint little hotel that was highly recommended by other cruisers. It was clean and very safe. Ellie could speak enough Spanish to get by and the locals just loved her. The women went a little overboard on their purchasing. Our rooms were full of stuff by the time we were ready to leave. Tom and I put the girls in the back seat and proceeded to stack stuff in their laps and between them. Every time we stopped on the way back to Puerto La Cruz, it took ten minutes to unload enough stuff to let them out. These two women boosted Merida's economy by at least two points all by themselves. They really did buy some neat stuff for the money, but this was ridiculous.

Tom was the navigator, so I blamed it all on him, when we got lost in Caracus. Somehow we took the wrong turn and were heading the wrong way. We were going through a tunnel and just the other side I saw a place to turn around and I went for it. Nothing was coming the other way so it looked like the right thing to do. Ellie had been calling me "Kamikaze" for days. I thought I would do something to live up to my nickname. I pitched the little Fiat into a slide and grabbed second gear. I had intentions of sliding it around this turnaround. But, the thieves around Caracus will steal anything and they had stolen the cover off a manhole right where we were turning around. I saw it too late. The right front wheel slid into it with a big bang. Scratch one wheel and tire and no telling what else. My stomach was doing flips. I got out and looked around. We did not need to be disabled in this area. I opened the door and helped Ellie to slip out from under the stuff and told her to get behind the wheel. Tom and I were going to have to lift the front end of the car while she backed up. Tom is not a big guy and I have a bad back. Frightened people have been known to have super-human strength. It was hard to believe but we lifted it up out of the manhole. We unloaded the trunk and changed the tire in record time. We needed to get out of there and fast. I wasn't sure the car was driveable. Thank God it was all right. It pulled to the right but it was moving. Everybody intently watched the road signs the rest of the way.

We'd only been back a couple of days from the Merida trip, when Tom, Ellie, and Elaine started hammering on me to charter a small plane for a trip to Angel Falls. At over 3000 feet, Angel Falls is the highest waterfalls in the world. Small planes have never appealed to me, especially a Venezuelan plane that was probably held together by bailing wire and duck tape. My nerves hadn't gotten over the Merida trip yet. They hounded me for a couple more days until I finally gave in. We flew out at first light for a three hour flight inland to the Canaima area. The pilot spoke good English and had flown for Avenza, a major airlines, for several years before he started his own chartering company. The Canaima area is one of the most primitive, unspoiled and beautiful areas on earth. As we approached it, we could see the tabletop mountains, called tepuies, rising up several thousand feet out of the jungle. It was the most amazing sight I had ever seen. I was already glad they had talked me into going.

Tom, Ellie, Elaine and I ready for takeoff.

A tepui (table top mountain) has its own endemic plant life; that is, they grow only there. Very few of the tepuis have been touched by the human foot.

We flew through the canyons right up next to the vertical walls. It was one breath taking view after another. We flew between two vertical walls into a canyon and, as the pilot put the plane into a hard turn, there it was right there in front of us--Angel Falls in full view. The pilot pushed the nose of the plane down and put us in a dive so that we could see the very bottom. The rainbows from the mist were phenomenal. I had seen pictures of Angel Falls in National Geographic but seeing it up close and in real life, was more special than I could imagine. The pilot said we were lucky there had been a lot of rain, that there usually wasn't this much water running off. He said man had never set foot on top of most of these tepuies, that they were inaccessible except by helicopter. He said it was almost impossible for researchers to get permits to explore this area.

Salto Angel (Angel Falls) in Canaima

Canoes the guides used to transport us to more waterfalls.

We landed on an airstrip cut out of the jungle. The government had supervised trips with guides to see some more of the fantastic waterfalls. Part of the trip was by canoe--the rest was by hiking through the jungle. The young gentleman who was our guide could speak five languages. He was very bright and entertaining. I was curious as to his education and how much he makes. He said he had his masters degree from the University of Miami and he made the equivalent of about 200 U.S. dollars a month. He felt very fortunate to have such a good paying job.

The guide sure earned his pay with us. These guides take everyone under massive waterfalls. Tons of water fall on you. It was a challenge just to walk without being knocked down. Elaine, being a non-swimmer, did not know to take one hand and hold it over the nose so she could breath. She just quit breathing and thought she was going to die. When she did breath, she was breathing water. It scared the guide half to death and he rushed her out from under the falls. I don't know who was the most scared, him or Elaine.

Elaine, soaked and happy she is alive, pointing to the waterfalls that almost drown her.

Elaine and Ellie caught red-handed with their buddies.

Tom and I caught Elaine and Ellie flirting with two young "macho" men. The girls said we were nuts, that they'd hardly said a word to those two guys. Pictures speak louder than words or something like that. Anyway, the more jealous we acted, the better they liked it.

We flew out late in the afternoon and arrived back at the airport after dark. On the way back in the taxi, I told the gang I was glad I let them talk me into going. It was definitely one of the best things I had ever done. The other major trip we took was to the Orinoco Delta area to visit the Warao Indians. We took this trip with some friends from Michigan, Todd, Nancy and their son David. We took a canoe through an Amazon-like area to where the Warao Indians lived like they did hundreds or maybe thousands of years ago. Monkeys were playing in the trees above us. Crocodiles lay on the banks. We fished for and caught piranha.

Father and son in their canoe.

I caught one, look closely.

The Warao Indians lived on the banks of the river in open, thatch-roof sheds. They slept in hammocks and their main food was iguanas. We stopped and visited one family. The guide showed us some beautiful balsa wood carvings of animals and canoes. We purchased some for two U.S. dollars each. My mind started working. The guide said all the Indians were good carvers and it only took about an hour to carve one of these pieces. I told the guide to tell the lady that I would buy all the carvings they could do for two dollars each. If each one of them would do five carvings a day they could each make ten dollars a day. The lady looked at me and laughed. The rest of the Indians started giggling. The lady waved her arm back and forth at her home and said they did not need any more money, they had everything they needed. They appeared to be totally content and happy.

Home Sweet Home

One of the larger homes, it had a couple of tables.

We flew home in late March. The bottom of Jaibolero was sand-blasted and he was left on the hard at Puerto La Cruz. It was their dry season and the humidity was very low. After three months of drying time, I flew back down to supervise the new epoxy bottom job. I had to get Jaibolero back in the water and all cleaned and waxed before Elaine and her friends arrived. I worked about 12 hours a day for three weeks and it was worth it. Jaibolero looked great.

The ten days the girls were with us were absolutely great. The first night we took a cab and went to downtown Puerto La Cruz for dinner and some sidewalk shopping. The cab driver grinned at me and said, "Harem." I said, "Si." The girls were real sports. They were my harem for the next ten days.

How do you keep hillbilly women happy? Give them a couple dollars and turn them loose on Paseo Calon in Puerto La Cruz to buy jewelry.

My "harem" at a fishing village in Mochima.

We did some island hopping. The girls snorkeled and worked on getting a good tan. We sailed to Mochima, a quaint little fishing village known for their restaurants. After a fantastic dinner of fresh fish, we had a nice little walk through town before going back to the boat.

The girls were tough. Not a one of them got sea sick. They were having a ball. Typical of women, they couldn't wait to get to Margarita for the "super-bowl" of shopping. There was one problem on board. It was something of a challenge for four women to get ready to go out with only one bathroom.

Late Monday afternoon we stopped by the telephone company so everyone could call home. I received the bad news that my father had passed away the night before. He had been very sick and weak for years. This produced a real challenge of how to get back home for the funeral and where to leave the boat. The girls had reservations to fly from Margarita to Caracas to the U.S. on Wednesday. On Wednesday and Saturday there was one direct flight from Margarita to Miami. The Wednesday flight had been booked for months and had over 40 people on the waiting list. All of the flights from Margarita to Caracas were full with long waiting lists. On top of all that, there were rumors that the F.A.A. was going to stop all flights from Venezuela to the U.S.

It was Tuesday morning and I was desperate. I stopped by a travel agency and asked for the manager. I told him my problem and asked for his advice. He said he would put one of his girls on the computer and keep her there until we got on the flight. If there were any cancellations, he would see to it that our names were inserted before anyone else. Finally, late Tuesday, they got us on Wednesday morning's flight.

I was fortunate that a friend, Ed on Willpower, was going to be in the anchorage for a couple of weeks and said he would keep an eye on Jaibolero. Elaine and I flew to Miami and then on to Atlanta. We were supposed to fly from Atlanta to Nashville on the 6 PM flight but got bumped to the 8 PM flight. We also got bumped on the 8 PM flight. I was livid. The last flight to Nashville was at 10 PM. I told the Delta Airlines management my situation and that we'd better be on the next flight. They assured us we would be.

At about 9 PM, Elaine said the girls' flight was supposed to arrive about 9:20. She suggested that we go to their gate and surprise them as they got off the plane. When we got to the gate, we were surprised to find Peggy's husband, Frank, there waiting. Frank, an attorney, had flown in from Washington to meet the girls and drive them to Kentucky. The girls had driven to Atlanta and left the car at my nephew's house to fly to Venezuela. The plane arrived and people started getting off the plane. The last few people left the plane and still no girls. I told Frank they had so many carry on bags of gifts and things that it would take a little while to get everything together. Frank was looking worried. Finally, the stewardesses came walking past us. I asked if anyone else was on the plane, she said she hoped not.

Frank and I immediately headed for the phones. I called Delta and found out that they had missed their connection in Miami. Elaine said that they had a long layover in Miami and wouldn't have missed their flight unless something made the flight from Caracas real late. I called the Venezuelan airlines and found out that the F.A.A. had indeed stopped all flights out of Venezuela to the U.S. It looked like the girls were stranded in Venezuela.

After several more calls, we learned there was one flight from Caracas that had made it to Miami. There were usually several flights each day so there was a slim chance they had gotten out. Frank finally learned there were three U.S. citizens on that one flight. Our persistence paid off, the girls were on the flight and were in a hotel in Miami.

What the girls went through that day was one scary story. It was obvious that the Venezuelan airlines were really ticked off at the U.S. and that included any of its citizens. The girls were in the wrong spot at the wrong time. They were herded into a room, separated from the other passengers and locked up. They were interrogated and searched. It must have really been a terrifying ordeal to experience. Somehow, they got on the only flight that day to the U.S. Several other U.S. citizens, who had booked flights that day, were not as fortunate. When the girls arrived in Miami the TV stations and the news reporters were there to interview the last U.S. citizens out of Venezuela. It's obvious that the Venezuelan officials picked these three frightened and hysterical women as an example, showing how U.S. citizens will be treated if the F.A.A. doesn't get off their backs. I could imagine the three of them all talking at once to the reporters. They definitely had a story to tell.

We made the 10 PM flight to Nashville and our son was waiting to drive us to Owensboro. Everyone was surprised we got home in time for the funeral with all the trouble the Venezuelan airlines was having with the FAA. The two governments got things worked out and we were able to fly back to Margarita after a couple weeks. We sailed back over to Puerto La Cruz. Venezuela is one of the most beautiful countries in the world and we saw a lot of it in the time we were there. Our visas were running out again so we decided to head west. In a way we hated to go because we had made friends with some super people. The "good-byes" were tough but we were looking forward to seeing Isla Tortuga, Los Roques, and the Avies before heading further west to the ABC's (Aruba, Bonaire, and Curacao).

Our friends, Edwin and Peggy, on Soleil Bleu.

Chapter 17

Venezuela to Miami

It was Saturday, September 26, 1996, and we were anchored at Dos Mosquises in the archipelago of Los Roques. Los Roques was about seventy miles off the coast of Venezuela and consists of over 300 islands and cays protected by an arc-shaped barrier reef, 14 by 25 miles. It looked like it should be in the South Pacific. Cruising boats could only stay for 14 days. There was no place to get water or supplies or to get rid of your trash. It was beautiful and pristine and the people in charge worked hard at keeping it that way. There were some 80 species of birds and the fishing was as good as it gets. There were seemingly an infinite number of coral reefs loaded with fish of all kinds and all it took were snorkel, mask and flippers to see one of the most beautiful things God has ever created.

We were sitting in Jaibolero's cockpit looking at an island with beautiful white sand beaches and palm trees. The trade winds were furnishing a nice breeze and the water colors were phenomenal. Our friends Larry and Linda on Niele were anchored beside us. The pelicans were fishing. Everything was utterly peaceful. Then I got this urge to write. It had been several months since I'd had this strange urge. Why would anyone want to sit down below with their head buried in a computer when they could be walking the beach, snorkeling, fishing, wind surfing or relaxing with a good book. It must have been a kind of sickness.

When we first started cruising, I wrote nearly every day about our escapades, mostly describing the many times we ended up in one of those predicaments where we could have lost our boat and, maybe, our lives. I wrote ten chapters of the *"Saga of the Sailing Hillbillies"* and I had several other chapters outlined. This writing thing was beginning

Larry and Linda on Niele.

to control my life. I was planning everything around the writing. I was waking up at all hours of the night and going to the computer, rewriting this thing that started out as a joke. I never intended to try to write a book. The sailing club back home had a monthly newsletter and I was just trying to contribute. It had possessed my subconscious and my subconscious mind would not let my conscious mind or my body rest. There was no way I could enjoy cruising and at the same time, write this stupid thing. I felt that Elaine was about ready to quit cruising because we had stopped having fun. Its like we were either struggling for our lives or I was writing. No telling how many times we were asked to do something with some other cruisers but couldn't because I had to write. You would have thought that I was working on a great novel and had to meet a deadline or something.

It may just be a coincidence but after I quit writing we stopped getting into these life-threatening predicaments. Because of this, Elaine accuses me of creating these situations so I would have something to write about. I would never admit to anything so ludicrous but I agreed that it did look suspicious. Anyway, I was starting to figure this cruising thing out. I quit trying to "second guess" the weatherman and I started reading the cruising guides and heeding their warnings. I started listening to the cruising nets on single side band and to other cruisers that had "been there and done that." Elaine had never listened to the weather before, now she never misses it. We could listen to the same weather report and hear two different things. She said my optimistic mind distorted things to what I wanted to hear.

Fourteen days just wasn't long enough in the Roques. We could have stayed fourteen months if supplies had been available. The next stop just west of the Roques was the Islas de Aves, another horseshoe reef with two islands and a few smaller cays. The main attraction here is the red-footed booby. This is a bird, not an American sunbather who forgot to put lotion on her feet. There were thousands of the boobies nesting when we were there. Their chicks are snow white and fluffy with bright red feet. They were unintimidated by humans and we could dingy within a few feet of their nests in the mangroves. The boobies aren't the only thing worth mentioning on the Aves. This place has the biggest, scariest fish I have ever seen.

Elaine and I went snorkeling. I was diving for lobster about one hundred yards from the dingy. Elaine had gone in the other direction. I came up for air just in time to see Elaine levitating into the dingy. She has never been able to get in the dingy without my help. I knew something must have really been frightening for her to fly into the dingy that way. I swam back as fast as I could. Elaine screamed for me to get out of the water, that there was a ferocious-looking fish chasing her and that it was bigger than the dingy. I put my mask on and did not see anything. I dove under to the other side of the dingy and, there it was, about twenty feet away and looking at me. I leaped into the dingy, pulled anchor and got out of there!

We immediately went and told Larry and Linda what we had encountered. I told them it looked like a ten to twelve-foot barracuda and its head had to be eighteen inches wide. They just laughed and said there is no such thing as a barracuda that big. Larry said that our hillbilly imaginations were running wild again. That night I looked through my fish books and, sure enough, there is such a thing as a great barracuda. They get to be ten feet in length. I couldn't wait to show Larry.

The next morning I was in the cockpit having coffee watching the boobies when Linda dove in for her morning swim. The next thing I heard was this blood curdling scream and Linda trying to get up the ladder. She finally got on board and collapsed. I yelled over and asked, "Are you all right?" She raised up and looked at me with eyes as big as silver dollars and said, "It's down there under our boat." I asked, "What's down there?" She said, "A giant barracuda." I started to comment that it was her Honolulu imagination running wild but I didn't. We were out of bread and fresh vegetables and no one wanted to get in the water any more, so we sailed west to Bonaire.

There was just one small area where cruisers can anchor on the leeward side of Bonaire and that was on a sandy shelf near the town dock. The Bonaire government has put down several moorings along this shelf for cruisers to use and help save the coral. The coral attracts the sea life and this attracts the divers. The diving business and tourism are the backbone of their economy.

The waters around Bonaire were phenomenal. Diving just doesn't get any better than the diving on Bonaire. I had carried my dive gear on board for two years and had only made a couple of dives. I made twelve dives the month we were there.

At certain times of the year there weren't enough moorings for all the cruisers. We had to anchor in the designated area and wait for a mooring to become available. The holding in this area was not the best, about 6 inches of sand over a rock bottom. There was room to put out just one anchor. I was a little worried but it held the first night. I hopped in the dingy the next morning and went to the marina about a mile away to pick up a fax. I left Elaine on Jaibolero reading a book. There were some cruising friends at the marina who we hadn't seen for months so I visited with them for about 30 minutes. When I started back to Jaibolero I saw a sailboat way off shore. It never dawned on me that it could be Jaibolero because Elaine was on board. The closer I got to the anchorage the more I realized that the boat way out there was my boat and I couldn't see anyone in the cockpit. This scared me because I thought something had happened to Elaine. The wind had picked up a little and Jaibolero had drifted far enough from the lee of the island that the waves made for a rough dingy ride. Finally I reached Jaibolero and yelled for Elaine. She climbed up in the cockpit and asked what was wrong. She then looked around and realized what had happened. She had fallen asleep and didn't know that the anchor had dragged and that she was floating out to sea. It's a good thing I didn't stay and visit for a hour or two. We went back and anchored again. I found someone who was leaving the next day and arranged to get their mooring.

Bonaire was really neat in that cruisers can take their dinghies right up a small channel next to the airport terminal, pick up their guests and dingy back to the boat. It was the only place we had seen where this could be done. Not only do you save a lot of money on taxi fares, it was just a neat thing to do.

Our friends from Miami, David and Pat and their son Michael, who was teaching in Caracas, visited us for a week of diving, fishing and sight seeing. David was an Owensboro native and we ran around together in high school. We hadn't seen much of each other since then, until we started cruising. We are in and out of Miami a lot and try to see them when we can.

While David and Pat were there, we rented a little Suzuki van for some sightseeing. On a trip around the island, we stopped at a lake on the windward side that is famous for its windsurfing. Since David is not a windsurfer,

Good windsurfing form or what?

Pat modeling for a car rental agency.

I told David not to park so close to the beach.

I took the opportunity to demonstrate some championship techniques while hanging on a rope at the bar. David thought it was very thoughtful of the owners of the place to put ropes there for that very reason.

The main industry on Bonaire is the salt mines. I never really thought about it before but this is a good business. There is plenty of salt in the saltwater. The wind is always blowing, so use the windmills to pump the saltwater up in the flats. The sun is almost always shining, so use the sun to evaporate the water and the end result is salt. Just scrape it up into big piles and ship it.

We really enjoyed the island tour, especially the flamingos. Bonaire is famous for its flamingos. Of course, Bonaire is also famous for its fishing and, since David and Pat are avid fishermen, we chartered a boat and Michael caught us supper. We arranged for a chef at one of the main beach hotels to prepare the fish along with some special seasoned vegetables and asked several of the other cruisers for dinner. It was a feast and a really great time. Everyone said the meal was one of the best they had ever eaten.

Michael with the catch of the day.

I had been windsurfing a couple times a day for the last few weeks and was getting pretty good at it. I kept the board tied off behind Jaibolero. I would untie the board and windsurf to the south end of the island, about 6 to 8 miles, and back and never get my trunks wet. The winds were between 10 and 15-knots every day and I was anxious and ready (I thought) for stronger winds. I really wanted to go faster. One afternoon it looked like a little storm was brewing and the winds picked up. This was my opportunity. I told Elaine I was going windsurfing and for her to check on me every once in a while. If the winds got too high or if I injured myself, she would have to come and get me in the dingy or I could end up out to sea.

At about 20-knots the winds were about all I really wanted. I was flying across the bay. The winds kept increasing and I fell more often. The higher the wind speeds, the harder it was to pull the sail up and get started again. I was really looking good, pulling way back and flying, when all of a sudden a strong gust hit me and I flew over the sail. I instantly knew I had hurt my back. I was a long way from the boat but I could tell Elaine was not in the cockpit. I waited and waited and was just drifting further and further out to sea. After several minutes, I had drifted out so far that I couldn't tell if she was in the cockpit or not. She had probably dozed off while reading, as usual. I tried several times to get the sail back up but my back hurt too badly. The wind kept blowing me further out to sea. I could hardly see the boat. By now, I was far enough away from the lee of the island that the waves were getting huge. I wasn't sure I could windsurf in these waves even if the wind did die down. There wasn't but one thing left to do. It was time to dump the sail and lay down on the board and try to paddle back in with my arms. The mast would not release from the pivot, it was stuck. I couldn't pull with enough force with my back the way it was. I was twisting and pulling as hard as I could and my hand slipped. I now had a nasty cut on the palm of my left hand to attract the sharks.

I knew Elaine would wake up sooner or later and get a search party to come looking for me. It was going to be pitch dark in another thirty minutes. Finally the winds let up a little. I had stretched some and my back was feeling better. My hand would not stop bleeding. It was only a matter of time before the sharks showed up. My only chance was to sail this thing back. I gave it one more try and slowly pulled up the sail and took off again. The waves were at least six feet high--I would never have even dreamed I could windsurf in these conditions. I had to tack back and forth into the wind and waves for a long way to get back to the boat. If I fell, I don't think I could have gotten back up again. It was not a matter of form or going fast, to stay up was to survive. I made up my mind that if I made it back, I was going to trade in my

"Type A" personality for something a little more conservative. I could understand kids out testing their limits but, I was no spring chicken anymore, and I had pressed my luck way too far, way too many times. I don't know how but I made it to Jaibolero. Elaine was down below reading and forgot about checking on me. I was too thankful for having made it back to be mad at her. My back hurt but I felt good inside just knowing that I had gotten back by myself. My back hurt for months. Windsurfing aggravates a bad back so I finally sold my windsurfer. My dream of being the best 60 year old windsurfer in the world was history.

We left Bonaire the end of October and sailed west to Curacao. We left Jaibolero anchored in Spanish Waters, an inland bay, and flew home for Thanksgiving and stayed until after the first of the year. While we were home, we decided to sail Jaibolero back up to the Virgin Islands for the spring. Several of our cruising friends were leaving Venezuela, Margarita, Bonaire, and Trinidad and were going back up to the Virgins. Our original plans were to keep going west to the Bay Islands off Honduras, then to the Rio Dulce in Guatemala and to the barrier reef off Belize before sailing back up to Florida. We will definitely visit these places but probably in 1998.

To sail back up to the Virgins, we needed to get further east, at least to the Roques, before we could head north so that we would be at a better point of sail. In addition to the current, the predominate winds in January are from just north of east in the 15 to 20-knot range. Most cruisers leave Curacao or Bonaire and drop down to the Venezuelan coast and motor day and night for a couple of days to get to Margarita before they head north. The counter current and winds tended to help along the coast, especially at night. The other option was to bite the bullet and head into the trade winds and current and motorsail over to the Roques. We caught a couple of days with winds less than 10 knots, so we took the second option.

We staged ourselves at the east end of the Roques and waited for a weather window. After a couple of days Herb (Southbound II), the weatherman, predicted the trade winds (Christmas winds) would ease up for the next two days. We pulled anchor about 4 PM and headed east. I wanted to get about 80 miles further east before we went north.

With any luck, we would be able to head north about noon the next day.

The longest we had ever been out before was for just one night and this was going to be a four-day crossing. I had been looking forward to a major crossing for a long time. I was excited, Elaine was worried. This had to be a good trip or I would never get Elaine to make another crossing. My luck had not changed. By 9 PM we were in the middle of a bad squall with 40 to 45-knot winds from the east and some very heavy rain. I saw it coming and shortened sail in time. We continued motoring into the wind and waves. Elaine was not a happy camper, she wanted to turn around and go back. I told her it would blow through, that it was just a squall. She said I told her the same thing on our first overnight sail and that storm lasted for 30 hours. Thank God the storm blew through in about an hour, but the seas were still big and on our nose. I put out more sail and started fighting our way east again. Before the night was over, we were hit by several more squalls. By 9 AM we had only made about 20 miles easting and I was beaten up and tired. Needless to say, Elaine was not happy with my choice of routes.

I decided to head north. It was stupid to try to head east in these conditions. We turned north to try and get out of the squally conditions. It was a good decision because, by 2 PM, the wind was less than 10 knots and the seas were laying down. By 6 PM there was hardly a white cap and we were doing 7 knots pinching the wind and heading straight for St. Thomas. I told Elaine that, if these weather conditions held up for three days, we would be in St. Thomas by Thursday evening and we would sail there on a single tack. The true wind speed stayed around 10 knots and the relative wind speed about 15 knots for the next three days--we never even started the engine. The solar panels and the wind generator kept the batteries up. The sea conditions were so perfect I hardly ever adjusted the sails or the autopilot. We caught the only good three-day window from January through March of 1997. All of our friends missed the window and everyone of them took a beating. We were very lucky.

We cruised the Virgins for the next couple of months. Our youngest son Jason and his girl friend came down for spring break. My cousin Kay and her husband Mike came down for a week. It was a great two months. Finally, it was decision-making time. Do we leave Jaibolero in the Virgins or do we sail him back up to Florida? Florida won the toss, because we had a new grandson and our other daughter-in-law was expecting twin boys. We knew we would be busy for the next several months and thought it best to have Jaibolero closer to home.

It usually takes eight or nine days of non-stop sailing from St. Thomas to make Miami. We planned on doing it in three legs--three days to the Turks and Caicos, two more days to Rum Cay and three more days to Miami. The Christmas winds were still blowing from the northeast and the seas on the north side of Puerto Rico were really bad. We decided to sail on the south side of Puerto Rico around to Boqueron and wait for a weather window. We had to wait two days at Boqueron before Herb, the weatherman, felt we had a decent weather window for the trip to the Caicos. Herb usually talks to about 80 cruisers each day. He helps boats crossing the Atlantic, cruisers in the Caribbean and in the Gulf of Mexico. Several hundred more listen in each day because he always talks to someone in each area and his predictions are the best a cruiser can get. Herb tends to be a little too conservative for me. However, I usually won't risk a crossing if he flat-out tells me not to go. Herb felt we had a three day window before the next front, so we pulled anchor and took off.

Herb was about 95 percent right. We made it to within about 8 miles of Ambergris Islands, our destination in the Caicos, before the sky fell on us. It was about 4 PM and the winds had increased from 15 knots to above 30 knots and the seas were building. The anchorage was behind Big Ambergris Island but to get there, we had to navigate a few miles of the most dangerous waters we had seen. I had been through this area before and remembered dodging numerous elkhorn coral. It was pretty bad in calm weather. In horrible sea conditions and bad light, it was going to be very dangerous.

After checking the headings on the compass, the GPS waypoints and Van Sant's directions for getting through the coral, I lined up everything perfectly and started in. This mine field of coral was about as bad as it gets. It was raining, so I let Elaine stay down below dry and comfortable. In the trough of the waves I could see elkhorn sticking up on my left and on my right. I rechecked my position. It looked like we were heading in the right direction. We went about another half mile and, all of a sudden, I could see elkhorn coral everywhere. I yelled for Elaine to come up and help me find a way through this mess. We couldn't find a way through so I turned Jaibolero around. Elaine screamed for me to stop. There was coral all in front of us. I looked to the left and right and behind us. We were completely surrounded by coral. My stomach was doing flips. This time I just knew Jaibolero was going down. Elaine was up at the bow in the rain, wind and waves, hanging on for her life. She looked back at me and had that "deer in the head light" look that I've seen before. I yelled and told her she had to find a way back through this mess. It was time to do a little negotiating with the Lord. I told Him that if He got us through this safely, I would do anything He asked. All He had to do was ask and I would do it. Elaine went to work and started pointing in the direction I needed to point Jaibolero. I'm sure she was praying, too. We zig-zagged back and forth just missing coral several times. I'm not sure if it was her praying or my bargaining or both but something worked. We had some very close calls but we finally got through and out in deeper water.

We considered our options, sail for a couple more days in bad seas or try to find our way back through the coral to the safe anchorage. The winds were letting up a little, but they were still pretty bad. I told Elaine I thought we could pick our way through if she stayed on the bow and gave directions. We had enough daylight left for one more try. It was her call. The Admiral had to make a tough decision. She pointed to the anchorage. I told her, "that's my girl, do a Floyd and go for it." It wasn't easy, but we made it through. There were some very close calls. After we got anchored I told her that I wasn't worried one bit. I told her she had S.P.P. She was not in a joking mood but her curiosity got the best of her and asked what it meant. I told her that S.P.P. was "super prayer power."

The next morning the winds were about 20 knots from the east so I pulled anchor early and we made great time sailing across the Caicos banks to Providenciales. We stayed at Provo a couple of days waiting for Herb to give us a good weather window. It is about a day and a half sail from Provo to Rum Cay. Elaine said that she was not going to give the pull anchor command until we had at least a three-day window.

For once I agreed with her. I don't think my nerves could have taken any more excitement. Herb finally told us just what we wanted to hear. We pulled anchor and planned on stopping at Rum Cay the next day. Because we were having such a good sail and the weather was so great, we went on to Nassau.

We dropped anchor just as the sun went down. While we were sailing into Nassau, Elaine heard Herb say that a nasty front was heading for the Bahamas. It should be in Nassau in 24 to 36 hours. The local weather predicted winds from the southeast in the 20 to 25-knot range for the next 24 hours. About noon the next day we were heading back to Jaibolero in the dingy with supplies when this strong urge hit me to pull anchor and try to beat the storm to Miami. I told Elaine to hurry up and put things away, that we were going to Miami. She told me that I could take her to shore, that she would fly to Miami and meet me there. For once I really knew this was the right thing to do. I guaranteed her we would be in Miami in 24 hours and have dinner with our friends, Dave and Pat. The food trick usually worked. It sounded good, eating out and everything, but she shook her head no. After pleading with her for several minutes, she finally gave in. I knew, however, that if that storm caught up with us out there on the banks, we were in deep trouble. She said that this was my last chance, that if I was wrong, to forget about her going cruising ever again. I knew she didn't really mean it.

The race was on, Jaibolero and I against the weather gods, we were going to win this time. With 25 to 30 knots of wind on the rear quarter the whole way across the banks, we flew. We surfed above maximum hull speed the whole way. In fact, we went too fast. When we got to the Cat Cay/Gun Cay Cut, it was still dark and we had to drop anchor for a couple of hours and wait for daylight before we could make the cut. Elaine took the anchor watch and made sure we didn't end up on the rocks.

At first daylight, she woke me and we headed across the Gulfstream to Miami. We made great time until we were about 12 miles off Key Biscayne. Elaine was down below sleeping and the winds died. I was stomping around, rolling in the sails, fussin' and cussin', when she came up in the cockpit. She looked at me like I was crazy and asked if I had totally lost it. She wanted to know if we were going to float around out there for two or three days or start the engine and motor on in. I told her I wouldn't expect her to understand what it meant to a sailor to return home after a three-year trip and come in under diesel power instead of sail. She just shook her head. She said it was a little anticlimactic but a lot better than the last time we returned with Hurricane Gordon nipping our heels. She was right again.

Chapter 18

Jaibolero Runs Off

One of my biggest fears while cruising was to leave my boat at anchor and have it not be there when I got back. To have the anchor drag and find out that my boat had taken off for parts unknown without me. I have always been extra careful to make sure my anchor was well set. I've always backed down in reverse until it grabbed and then given the boat more throttle to make sure it was absolutely set. I then put out the proper amount of scope (length of anchor rode divided by the depth). If there was any question about only one anchor holding, then I put out two. If the anchorage had questionable holding, I dove on the anchor to help it set. Every time I left Jaibolero I told him, "Do not go anywhere, stay put until I get back." This sounds superstitious but it always worked, except once.

Anchoring has cost me more sleep than anything else. No telling how many times I have awakened in a cold sweat and gotten out of bed to see if the anchor was dragging. I have had numerous nightmares about us going on the rocks. Even if the anchorage was calm as a duck's pond I got up three or four times a night to check things out. I not only worried about my anchor dragging, I worried about the other boats in the anchorage. I took a mental picture of the boats around us before I went to bed and made sure they were where they were suppose to be each time I got up. Charterers were the ones to watch out for. If a charterer anchored in front of me, I watched him real close and, if I thought they are not anchoring properly, I would pull anchor and move. Another thing I watched out for was the yo-yo that pulled up in the middle of an anchorage and put out two anchors when everybody else had one. If there was a change of wind direction in the middle of the night, everybody swung but him and this was a problem.

The single thing that has irritated me the most was for someone to put out way more scope than was necessary. Sometimes, you wouldn't find out until it was too late. In an anchorage about eight-feet deep, everyone should have out 50 or 60-feet of rode. Every boat swings on a 50 or 60-feet radius except for the jerk with 120 feet. We pulled into an anchorage on Isla Tortuga where I dropped anchor in seven feet of water and made sure that the anchor was set. I cut the engine off and started down below when I heard someone yell from the boat next to me. He told me in a rude way that I had anchored too close to him. I asked him how that could be because I was at least 90 to 100-feet from his boat. He said he had out 150 feet of chain. I told him that he had to be joking, that no one would put out that much anchor rode in seven feet of water. He proceeded to tell me in a strong accent that he was from Sweden and that he knew how to anchor. He said he was there first and that I had to move. I laughed at him and told him to crank in about 100 feet of chain and everybody would be all right. He insisted that I move. There was no way I was going to move.

The Admiral overruled my decision. A lowly Captain must obey and respect the chain of command. The Admiral hates conflict and was not going to stay anchored next to these people even though she knew we were in the right. I pulled anchor and moved. I told the Admiral that I had a game plan for this jerk. If the wind picked up that night, I was going to swim over and dive on his anchor and unset it and watch him take off dragging. She shot that down and accused me of having a bad attitude.

Even as conscientious about anchoring as I have been, I have had a few minor incidents, nothing serious except for one time. Elaine has kept after me to write about this very embarrassing incident that occurred at St. Johns in the Virgin Islands in the spring of 1997. I've told her time and time again that I did not want anyone to know about this incident. I didn't even want to think about it, much less, write about it. I told her that if she ever told anyone, I would make up something twice as embarrassing about her and tell the world. Her logic was that as I had told everything else about all my screw ups, I might as well tell about this. I told her the only person that never screws up, never does anything. I love the Bahamian t-shirt that says, "Nobody moves, nobody gets hurt." Show me a cruiser whose anchor hasn't dragged and I'll show you one that stayed in marinas and never used his anchor.

I finally gave in. I hate telling this but I guess I have to. Elaine says the "Saga" would not be complete without this story. So, here goes. Two couples that were friends of some of our cruising friends had rented a house with a pool on St. Johns. They invited several of us up to their house for a swim party. I told Elaine that we swam off the boat or went snorkeling almost every day. I could have cared less about swimming in a pool. It would be a lot of trouble for nothing. The Admiral pulled rank. We were all to meet at Cruz Bay, and get into one of those pickup truck taxis with all the benches and all go to the house together. We had been anchored in Francis Bay and since it was only four miles around to Cruz Bay, Elaine and I took Jaibolero. We anchored right outside Cruz Bay like we had done several times before with no problems. No storms or chance of bad weather was forecast. Sometimes we would be lucky and get on one of the moorings right around the corner but they were all taken this day. We dropped anchor in about 15 feet of water and backed down on it until it grabbed. I let out about 90 feet of chain rode which should have been sufficient. We backed down again and the anchor was set good. I don't know why but, when we were in the dingy and I looked back at Jaibolero, I had this real emotional feeling come over me. I told Elaine that I sure hoped he was going to be all right anchored there. She told me that I was being ridiculous, that we had anchored there several times before with no problems. The Admiral had spoken.

As we were pulling up to the dingy dock, I told Elaine I wished we weren't going. My veto was over-ridden as usual and we went to meet the others. We found a taxi big enough to haul us and the deal was negotiated. Somehow the directions got screwed up and we went in the wrong direction for about 20 minutes. After much discussion with the taxi driver, we started back to Cruz Bay to try another road. We were back tracking around the side of this hill while I was trying my best to get a glimpse of Jaibolero in the anchorage. There was a brief moment when I could see the anchorage but I did not see Jaibolero. My stomach lurched and tied itself into a knot. There were other boats there and a couple of them were large charter boats. I told myself they must have blocked my view of Jaibolero. We went a little further and I yelled for the taxi driver to stop. Everyone looked at me like I was nuts. I told them I was worried about Jaibolero, that I was going back to make sure he was all right. I told Elaine she could go on with the others, that they could bring her back to the boat when the party was over. She said she was going with me.

We ran through town to the dingy dock. Some other cruisers were there as we jumped into the dingy. They could tell we were upset and asked if something was wrong? I told them that I wasn't for sure and took off wide open through Cruz Bay Harbor. We rounded the corner and my feelings were right, Jaibolero was gone. To understand how I felt, just think about driving down the street to your home, the home that you truly love with all your belongings in it, pulling up in the driveway and your home is gone. We looked north towards the Windward Passage, west toward St. Thomas, and south through Pillsbury Sound. There was no Jaibolero to be seen. I gassed the dingy and went around the corner to Caneel Bay but still no Jaibolero. Elaine wanted to know what I was going to do next. Why do I always have to be the one to come up with the something to do next in crisis situations? There was a two to three knot current that runs between St. Thomas and St. Johns and there was no telling which way he went. It had been over an hour since we'd left him at anchor. The National Park Service headquarters was in Cruz Bay next to the dingy dock. We headed that way with hopes that they could help. They had high powered, twin-engine boats and that was what we needed to find Jaibolero.

The lady at the desk tried to raise the park rangers on the radio but not a one answered. She tried for several minutes with no luck and said it was highly unusual for her not to be able to reach somebody. I borrowed her VHF and called the Coast Guard. They said they would find someone to help but first I had to answer some questions. I answered a couple of questions and was put on hold because another call was coming in. There was no way I was going to stand there holding onto a VHF on hold while my boat was going further out to sea or onto the rocks somewhere.

I went outside and felt like I was going to get sick. Some guy came up and said he'd heard me talking to the Coast Guard. He said he was with the Rescue Squad and maybe he could help. I don't know how he knew I was the one who'd lost his boat. I guess it was written on my face. I said the only help I needed was a high powered speed boat so I could cover a lot of area fast. Elaine said we needed a boat like the one at the fuel dock. There were two young men at the fuel dock in a cigarette-type fishing boat with big twin Yamahas. I told the Rescue Squad guy I needed that boat so let's confiscate it. I couldn't believe it, but he said he would try. He pulled some kind of badge out and said it was an emergency, we needed a fast boat and asked if they would help. They told us to hop in. They had just paid for the fuel and we took off.

The seas were always rough in Pillsbury Sound between St. Thomas and St. Johns, but this day was a little rougher than normal. I could tell by the direction the boats were swinging at anchor that the current was running from south to north through the Windward Passage. I told the young man driving to head for the Windward Passage as fast as possible. After about ten seconds, I was regretting telling him to go wide open. We were airborne about half the time and, during the other half, were crashing into big waves. Something told me that we were going the wrong way. I told the driver to turn left and head for the islands off the north end of St. Thomas. Within a few minutes, I could just barely make out what I thought was a boat on the windward side of a rocky island at least three miles away. I could barely see it when it was on top of a wave, then it would disappear into the trough. We got closer and I could tell that it was a sailboat and that it was sideways, which meant it was drifting. It looked terribly close to the island. Finally, we got close enough to see that it was Jaibolero. Could we get there in time to save him? I caught myself praying that he would be all right but quickly stopped that because a person should never pray for a materialistic object. I believe in saving those prayers for life-threatening situations. In my case, I couldn't afford to waste any favors!

There was a slim chance that Jaibolero's anchor could grab on something and keep him off the rocks. The deep blue color of the water showed that there was deep water right up to the rocky shoreline. As steep as the rocky walls were on this island, it didn't seem likely that the anchor would save Jaibolero. It was obvious that getting from one boat to another in these waves was going to an acrobatic feat, especially for a 53-year old man with bad back and shoulders. But, the closer we got, the more it looked like we might have a chance to save him.

The game plan was for the driver to pull the bow up at an angle so I could grab a life line, then hit reverse and back away as quickly as possible. The rescue guy was supposed to push off as soon as I grabbed a life line so I wouldn't get trapped between the two boats and get smashed. As the bow of the fishing boat was going up and Jaibolero was going down, I reached out and grabbed hold of the life line. I wasn't sure what happened next but the rescue guy lost his balance as he tried to push off and we were both left hanging on the life lines. I screamed, "Reverse, reverse!" The bow of the fishing boat was coming up again and the waves were pitching the fishing boat into Jaibolero. We were going to get seriously injured if we didn't do something fast. I could hear the big Yamahas rumbling as they kicked up out of the water when the driver gassed them in reverse. Somehow, the rescue guy and I both flipped up over the life lines onto Jaibolero's deck at the same time. For a second we just stood there and looked at each other. We were both wondering how we did it. The fishing boat banged the side of Jaibolero. The driver throttled back and the engines went back into the water. The fishing boat backed away. I jumped into the cockpit and started the engine and told the rescue guy to take the helm. Then I went forward to get the chain and anchor up with the manual windlass. Thank God, we got there when we did. A few minutes later and Jaibolero would have been destroyed on the rocks.

A person can "if" themselves into a nut house. There were a lot of "ifs" that day that had to be just right or Jaibolero would have been destroyed. If the taxi driver hadn't gone the wrong way. If I hadn't had that funny feeling and been looking for him as we back tracked around that hill. If I hadn't gone back to check on him. If the rescue squad guy hadn't heard me on the VHF. If Elaine hadn't noticed the two guys in the high powered fishing boat at the fuel dock. If the two guys weren't ready to leave the fuel dock at the right time. If we hadn't gone in the right direction. If we hadn't flipped up over the life line when we did. That night we were anchored back at Francis Bay and Elaine made the statement that we were sure lucky that we found Jaibolero when we did and that I was lucky I didn't get smashed between the two boats. I told her, "What's meant to be will be. Everything that happens is for a reason. It is all just part of the big picture and everything always turns out for the best in the long run. If you believe in God, you have got to believe this. Besides that, everybody knows the Good Lord takes care of those that can't take care of themselves. We have absolutely nothing to worry about."

Conclusion

Elaine's Uncle Tommy, God rest his soul, couldn't have been more right about sailing. He may have exaggerated a little about him sailing for forty years and still not knowing 10 percent, but not much. We have been cruising for over three years and I now may know half as much as Uncle Tommy did. So, where does this put me? This puts me on a steep learning curve with plenty of challenges to look forward to. Every time I pull anchor and take off on a crossing I still get "butterflies." I love it. I love it. I love it. This is just one of the things that worries Elaine. Another major worry for her is my memory. She loves to tell people, "Floyd has learned a lot about sailing. His problem is remembering what he learns."

There were times on some of those crossings when the weather gods decided to turn on us and I was so tired and beat up that I could hardly keep my eyes open, when I've asked myself, is it really worth it? Why am I out here? Am I nuts or what? I could be home in a nice quiet bed getting a good night's rest and playing golf every day. Then I think about some of the sailing accomplishments of sailors like Robin Knox Johnson, about the toughness and determination it took to be the first to sail non-stop, single handed around the world. Months of being out there alone, the constant struggle just to keep the boat on course and afloat, especially with the equipment that was available in the early 60's. Quite frequently I have someone tell me how we are living their dream and how brave we are for doing it. They may think I'm brave, but I know better. I used to think I was kind of brave but this sailing thing has truly humbled me. If there is such a thing as a thousand-foot tower of courage, Robin Knox Johnson is up there above the 900-foot level and I am about three steps off the ground.

My memory is questionable at times but those crossings that tested my courage are vividly ingrained in my mind forever. The sea gods exposed this hillbilly to more strife than I bargained for. I am not the only seafaring adventurer to survive what can be described as a very brutal and wet purgatory to complete their journey. Survive is the key word--some didn't. This spark of threat has kindled the desire for adventurers through the centuries to rise up and face the challenges of the sea. A land-lubber can not be expected to understand the self-reward of a hard fought battle with the sea. You have to respect something to love it. The slow learner that I am, it took me a few times struggling to save our lives for me to learn to respect the awesome power of the sea. Only after a cruiser has felt fear in his gut for hours or sometimes days can he truly respect and therefore love the sea and its challenges.

In no way is the "Saga" meant to be a "how-to" book. If anything, it is a "what-not-to-do" book. Elaine is afraid that anyone who reads this would never go cruising. I hope she is wrong. I want to be an ambassador to sailing and the cruising life, not try and discourage people. My greatest reward would come from saving just a few cruisers from making some of the mistakes I made. It does seem that all I wrote about was our struggle to survive. The old saying, "You have to take a little bad along with the good," definitely applies to cruising. All that we have experienced has not dampened our desire for cruising. My feelings are that the positives out weigh the negatives a thousand to one. Elaine says my love for sailing and my constant need for a challenge distorts my logic. She says her scales tilt a little in favor of the positives and that she has seen enough negatives. I think she loves it almost as much as I do. She is just trying to keep me from taking any more unnecessary risks in the future. She has asked me to go one year without getting us in one of those situations where she has to pray our way out of it. It's not that she doesn't like to pray. She is afraid she has used up all her favors.

The Admiral's Viewpoint

When Floyd first suggested cruising as a way of life, of course, I had reservations. I had no idea what to expect. I had no idea that there were thousands of people out there, no different from us, living the cruising life. A lot of couples sold all their worldly belongings in order to buy their boat and go cruising. I didn't have the nerve to do that. The only way I could go was to keep a small house in Kentucky and be assured that I could go there anytime I wanted. As it turned out, we have been on the boat about half the time and home the other half, which has satisfied both of us.

Having married young and started our family at age nineteen, I have been a mother most of my life. It seems my main role in life has been that of a caretaker. The "empty nest syndrome" has proven to be the hardest part for me even though I know I would have had to contend with that even if we were at home all the time.

After spending our lives taking care of businesses and family we rarely had time for each other. However, we had managed to survive over thirty years of marriage and were quite happy together. I certainly did not want to do anything to "rock the boat." I thought about all kinds of things, like wouldn't it be terrible to get out on a boat together and find out we really didn't like each other after all, or that I hated cruising and he loved it, or that one of us would be seasick all the time. I could just see me going home and him continuing on single handed. Fortunately for us, it has worked out to our benefit. People talk about bonding a lot these days. Believe me, we feel "well bonded." I can't think of a better way to bond than to get out on a boat away from it all where you can spend really quality time together with few interferences. We also found time spent on board with our sons and friends to be priceless. How often does one have the opportunity to have their adult children or friends all to themselves for any length of time?

I am thankful my husband is an adventurer and keeps life exciting for us. I'm not much of a leader but I'm a good follower. I have trusted Floyd's judgement most of the time. However, I'm afraid some of our precarious predicaments have been a bit more than I bargained for. Floyd's approach to life has been to go at it 120 percent. If things don't go as planned, he works hard and almost always finds a solution that fixes things. This attitude worked well in the business world but not with Mother Nature. She is the boss, especially when contending with the weather and the ocean. We were struggling to survive. This whole Admiral thing started out as a joke but something had to be done. Floyd just could not hear a bad weather report, it was always going to be better than predicted. He was right sometimes but, the times he was wrong, we were hanging on for dear life. After being appointed Admiral and having the authority to make the final call, things certainly got a lot calmer on Jaibolero.

Not only is Floyd an adventurer, he is also a storyteller. He sees a good story in events that simply pass by most with no story seen. Sometimes he may embellish his stories a bit to make them more interesting but, I think most of the time, he tells them the way he remembers them. The "Saga" had little embellishment. It didn't need it. Our misadventures were unbelievable and exciting enough as they were.

I hate to admit it to Floyd but I do believe the good times far outnumber the bad. No one gets excited hearing about sunsets, walks on the beach, the island people and their culture, fishing, snorkeling, quality time together and camaraderie amongst cruising friends. These are the main ingredients of the cruising life and the "war stories" are simply the spice.

I am thankful for the insight God has given me. I had experienced the power of prayer prior to our cruising life. Without prayer and God's protection we would not be here. God promises protection for those who pray. Floyd was at the helm of Jaibolero when we surfed across the sand bar going into Destin but it was Jesus and his hands that lifted the boat, carried it across and allowed us to safely reach a protected anchorage. This is as real to me as this boat I am setting in and the pencil I am writing with. There were several other times that I felt the power of prayer protected us. I truly don't believe I could go cruising without this protection.

About the Author

Floyd Tapp was born and raised in Owensboro, Kentucky. Floyd does not have to his credit any books or novels. His writings have not appeared in any periodicals, anthologies, symposia or encyclopedias, except for one small article in the *Owensboro Messenger-Inquirer.* He does not belong to any scholarly, professional, literary or social organizations except the AARP. Floyd only (barely) speaks one language and that is with a strong Ohio Valley River accent. He does have experience suckering tobacco, shucking corn, selling women's shoes, stuffing newspapers, sacking groceries, hustling pool and pumping gas. A graduate of Brescia College with a degree in math and physics, he has worked in the aerospace field for McDonald Douglas and Boeing Aerospace Divisions. He worked in flight dynamics and controls on the Saturn/Apollo Missions. He was a professional motorcycle flat-track racer. He left the aerospace industry in 1972 to become an entrepreneur. He has owned a dozen successful businesses. After 35 years of indecisiveness, Floyd has pursued the career of a writer. Floyd and his wife of over thirty years, Elaine, started cruising on their sailboat in 1995. Their misadventures have supplied the material for them to collaborate on this book. When they are not cruising on their boat, they are back in Owensboro with Floyd wishing he was on the boat.

ORDER FORM

Fax Orders: (502) 926-4025

Postal Orders: Ahoy Publishing, Floyd Tapp,
2116 Cedar Street, Owensboro, KY 42301
Tel: (502) 926-1480

❑ Please send "The Saga of the Sailing Hillbillies" to:

Name: ______________________________

Address: ______________________________

City: ____________ State: __________ Zip: __________

Telephone: (__________) ______________________

Price: $10.95 per book, shipping included.

Sales tax: Please add 6% for Kentucky addresses

Payment:
❑ Check
❑ Credit Card:
❑ VISA ❑ MasterCard ❑ DISCOVER NOVUS ❑ AMERICAN EXPRESS Cards

Card Number: ______________________________

Name on card: ______________________________

Expiration Date: ________/________

ALLOW 3 TO 4 WEEKS FOR DELIVERY.